War Criminals in Canada

James E. McKenzie

Detselig Enterprises Ltd.
Calgary, Alberta, Canada

War Criminals in Canada
© James E. McKenzie

Canadian Cataloguing in Publication Data
McKenzie, James E.
  War criminals in Canada

    Includes index.
    ISBN 1-55059-109-6

    1. War criminals -- Canada. 2. War crime trials -- Canada. 3.
Trials (Crimes against humanity) -- Canada. I. Title.
D803.M34 1995   341.6'9   C95-910579-4

Publisher's Data

Detselig Enterprises Ltd.
210, 1220 Kensington Rd. NW
Calgary, AB   T2N 3P5

Detselig Enterprises Ltd. appreciates the financial support for
our 1995 publishing program, provided by the Department of
Canadian Heritage, Canada Council and the Alberta Foundation
for the Arts, a beneficiary of the Lottery Fund of the Government
of Alberta.

Cover Illustration and Design by Dean MacDonald

Printed in Canada

ISBN 1-55059-109-6   SAN 115-0324

*To My Mother
Naomi McKenzie*

ACKNOWLEDGEMENTS

I'd like to thank several people who helped me with this project. First and foremost, I'm grateful to Sol Littman, the Canadian representative of the Simon Wiesenthal Centre. He generously gave me access to his files and office facilities in Toronto, answered countless questions, and encouraged me to write this book.

I'd also like to thank six of my students at the University of Regina's School of Journalism and Communications, who helped immensely with the research and writing. Lisa Cook, Deb Hadley, Justin Kohlman, Brian Miller, Denise Psiurski, and Michelle Spencer contributed a great deal. Their individual work is recognized in the chapter notes at the end of the book.

Thanks also to the University of Regina, which gave me the time and facilities to work on this book during the summer of 1994 and throughout the 1994-95 academic year. In particular, I appreciate the support of Bryan Olney, director of the School of Journalism and Communications.

I'd also like to thank my publisher, Ted Giles of Detselig Enterprises Ltd., for his encouragement and support, as well as Detselig's managing editor, Tara Gregg, who edited the manuscript.

Finally, thanks to Portia Rese, who did the interpretive portraits featured in this book.

James E. McKenzie
1995

WHAT IS A WAR CRIMINAL?

The Criminal Code of Canada was amended in 1987 to include the following definitions:

Crimes against humanity: Murder, extermination, enslavement, deportation, persecution or any other inhumane act or omission that is committed against any civilian population or any identifiable group of persons, whether or not it constitutes a contravention of the law in force at the time and in the place of its commission, and that, at that time and in that place constitutes a contravention of customary international law or conventional international law or is criminal according to the general principles of law recognized by the community of nations.

War crime: An act or omission that is committed during an international armed conflict, whether or not it constitutes a contravention of the law in force at the time and in the place of its commission and that, at that time and in that place constitutes a contravention of the customary international law or conventional international law applicable in international armed conflicts.

Act or omission include attempting or conspiring to commit, counselling any person to commit, aiding or abetting any person in the commission of, or being an accessory after the fact.

CONTENTS

Days in Court

Some Final Cases

INTRODUCTION

Old Crimes, Old Men

Hundreds of thousands of European immigrants streamed into Canada after the Second World War. Most were decent people who had suffered greatly, and deserved the wonderful opportunity they were given to start new lives in a peaceful and prosperous new country.

But mingled in with this mass of newcomers were a certain number of immigrants who, perhaps, were not such fine and upstanding future citizens. They were suspected war criminals – people who allegedly had taken part in the Holocaust.

Some of them were said to have been gas chamber operators, firing squad members and others directly responsible for the killings. Others were said to have been cattle-car loaders, camp guards and the like, cogs in the immense and ghastly death machine. Still others were said to be quislings who turned against their fellow-countrymen and helped the Nazis round up Jews in occupied nations.

If what was said about these immigrants was true – and that was a big "if" – they did not belong in Canada. They belonged behind bars in Europe, where they had committed their crimes and where they should be punished for them.

But were such people actually in Canada, or was it just loose talk? If, in fact, they were here, how had they gotten into the country? And what should be done about them? These are some of the questions this book explores.

The subject of alleged war criminals in Canada has long been shrouded in speculation and mystery. This book is an initial attempt to pull some of the major themes and cases together over the 50-year history of the war criminals issue, but a lot more research needs to be undertaken.

There's no doubt that wartime Europe was full of agents of the Holocaust. There had to be a lot of them – tens of thousands, and perhaps even hundreds of thousands – in order to murder so many people. It's estimated that six million Jews died in the Holocaust, and perhaps an equal number of non-Jews. Assembly-line murder required a lot of "workers."

After the Allied victory, Europe's war criminals did everything they could to avoid apprehension and punishment. Some no doubt realized that coming to Canada was a good way to do that. The federal government made an effort to keep suspected war criminals out of Canada, but the screening system was inefficient, and once they were in the country, suspected war criminals had little to worry about.

The government certainly didn't go out looking for them. As long as they obeyed the laws of this country, and didn't flaunt the fact that they had done "dirty business" back home during the war, Canadian authorities left them alone.

There were many reasons for this, as we will see in coming chapters, but essentially it boiled down to this: both Conservative and Liberal governments, up to about 1985, were unwilling to go after them. The war was over, and events which happened during the war seemed remote. If a handful of people had slipped into Canada after having done certain unpleasant things on another continent in another era, so what? That was the attitude of the Canadian government for almost 40 years.

But one sector of Canadian society didn't go along with this "let sleeping war criminals lie" approach. Canada's Jewish community, and Jews around the world, insisted that all those who had taken part in the Holocaust should be hunted down and punished, no matter where they had ended up after the war, and no matter how many years had gone by.

Canadian Jews were outraged by the government's indifference to the possibility that Nazi war criminals might be living in this country. Soon after the war ended, they began speaking out on the issue, and usually they found the news media eager to report their comments.

As the years went by, Jewish spokesmen and the media kept the subject alive. Eventually, in the mid-1980s, the Jews succeeded in their campaign to force the government into action, and since then the government has spent tens of millions of dollars on the pursuit and prosecution of alleged Nazi war criminals.

In the pages which follow, you will read about many individuals who have been publicly identified as suspected war criminals, but a word of caution is in order. The title of this book, "War Criminals In Canada," is meant to refer to the overall subject matter being discussed, and should not be taken to apply to any individual.

As you will discover, a great many allegations have been made over the years, but a much smaller amount of proof has been offered. In some cases, the charges have been shown to be groundless, while in others, the allegations have remained unproven, which, under our system of justice, means the individuals are entitled to the presumption of innocence.

You might be surprised to learn that as we enter the second half of the final decade of the 20th century, the government is still actively pursuing Nazi war criminals in Canada, despite the fact that more than 50 years have passed since the end of the Second World War. Indeed, the government has indicated that it intends to keep on going for the foreseeable future, although most suspected Nazi war criminals in Canada must be dead by now, and the rest, very old.

This raises an interesting scenario. Suppose a case comes up in which a man can be shown beyond a reasonable doubt to have committed atrocities during the Second World War. Say he directly took part in the killing of hundreds of men, women and children.

Suppose that man has lived in Canada for almost 50 years, and he's been a model citizen. He's almost 90 years old now. Should this man be punished? If so, how? Or do you think the government should let him alone, and leave his punishment up to God?

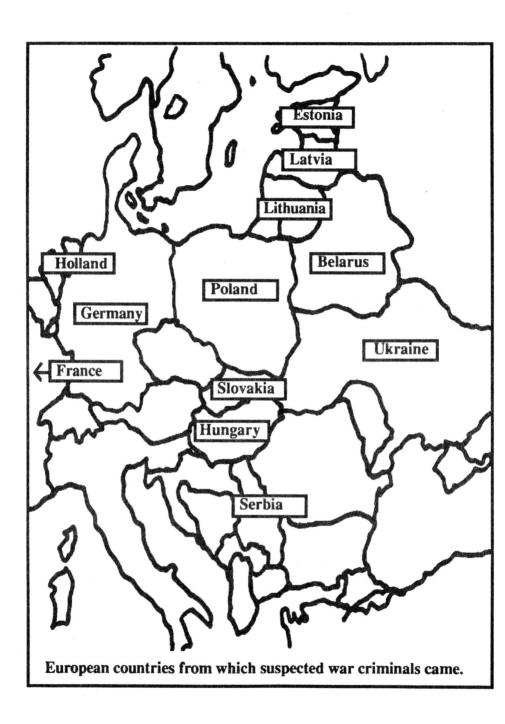

Estonia
Latvia
Lithuania
Belarus
Holland
Poland
Germany
Ukraine
France
Slovakia
Hungary
Serbia

European countries from which suspected war criminals came.

After the War

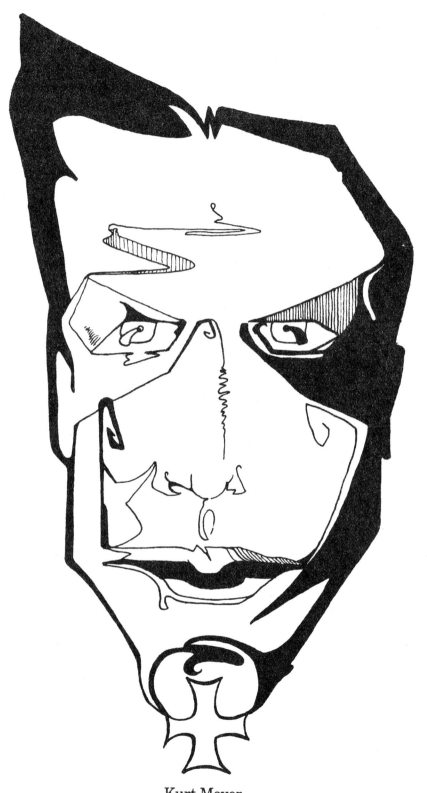

Kurt Meyer

CHAPTER 1

Murder In Normandy

Not all the Canadian soldiers who died during the Allied invasion of Normandy in June 1944 were killed in battle. At least 134 of them were murdered – gunned down by German soldiers who had taken them prisoner.

According to every principle of human decency and the rules of warfare agreed to by every civilized nation, including Germany, this was a crime. The Germans should have taken the Canadian POWs behind the lines, imprisoned them, and treated them decently. Instead, the German troops shot the Canadians down like dogs.

A few prisoners who managed to escape soon reported what had happened, and the Canadian Army vowed to punish the Germans responsible for these atrocities. But when the war ended less than a year later, none of the guilty parties was foolish enough to come forward and confess.

Army investigators couldn't identify even one German soldier who had personally taken part in the shootings.

The Army did, however, manage to get its hands on one of the officers who had been in command of the murderous German troops. And so Kurt Meyer became Canada's first war criminal.

Meyer had risen to the rank of brigadeführer (major-general) by the time he was captured in September 1944 and taken to England, where he was held until the end of the war. His high rank made him stand out, but he was not in the Wehrmacht, the regular German Army. Rather, he was a member of the Waffen

Schutzstaffel, the military wing of the SS, the black-uniformed Nazi elite which started out as Hitler's security guard and grew to become the most powerful and vicious arm of the Nazi regime.

The SS had been given primary responsibility for the eradication of Europe's Jews. Although Meyer wasn't involved in that, his SS affiliation made him evil personified in the eyes of many. In a sense, putting Meyer on trial was a way for Canada to put the SS on trial, and symbolically extract revenge for the evil the Nazis had unleashed on the world.

Meyer's trial before a Canadian Army court was Canada's version of the Nuremberg Tribunal, in which the victorious Allies brought the surviving senior Nazis to justice. As a junior partner in the war, Canada didn't rate a place at Nuremberg, but the trial of the SS major-general whose men had killed Canadian POWs in Normandy was a good substitute.

Kurt Meyer was born in 1910 near Berlin, the son of a factory worker. He became a police officer at the age of 19. In his off-duty hours, he was a motorcycle enthusiast and a show-off who broke 25 bones at different times in his life.

He joined the Nazi party in 1930. Six years later he joined the SS, which soon controlled all German police, security and intelligence services. When the SS developed its military wing Meyer became part of it. Thanks to his keen intelligence and leadership ability, he soon rose to become a senior officer.

Meyer was a good soldier. He won the Iron Cross, the Knight's Cross and several other medals. He served in Poland, the Balkans, Greece, Russia, Belgium and France, and he was decorated and praised by the Führer himself.

He was nicknamed Schnell (Speedy) Meyer because he was so aggressive in leading his men into action. After he became a tank commander he also became known as Panzer (Tank) Meyer.

He steadily rose in rank. By 1944, he had become a colonel and was in command of the 25th SS Panzer Grenadier Regiment, part of the Hitler Youth Division. By that point in the war the Germans were running out of fighting men, and most of the division's 21,000 troops were from 16 to 18 years old.

Meyer was only about 15 years older than they were, but he was a tough and experienced commander noted for his impassioned speeches to his young troops. He stressed the need for them to be loyal to Hitler and the Fatherland, and to deliver an all-out effort to win the war.

Meyer was also noted for his strict discipline. This took on great importance later, when, in an effort to escape responsibility for the murders of the POWs, he claimed his impulsive young troops killed the Canadian prisoners without his knowledge and consent. This was hard to believe, given the high level of discipline he imposed.

Meyer's regiment was part of the front-line force desperately trying to repel the Allies in Normandy. Soon after D-Day, Meyer's troops came up against Canadian soldiers near the towns of Bayeau and Caen. The fighting was fierce, and many Canadian troops were captured by the Germans.

Some of those POWs ended up being taken to a place near Meyer's field headquarters, which was in a small church known as l'Ancienne Abbaye Ardenne. That's where they were murdered. Thus it was hard to believe Meyer later when he claimed he knew nothing about it. It happened so close to his headquarters that he would likely have heard the shots.

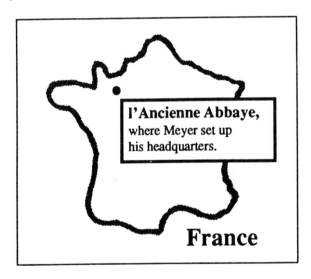

After these killings, the Hitler Youth Division was nicknamed the "murder division" by the Canadian troops in France. While the battle continued, Allied planes dropped leaflets telling about the murders of the Canadian prisoners, and promising punishment at the end of the war for those who had been responsible. It was a propaganda technique to dishearten the German soldiers, but it was also a promise which was eventually fulfilled by the post-war prosecution of Meyer.

As the Allied troops pushed deeper into France, and then on into Belgium and the Netherlands, Meyer's regiment and other parts of the Hitler Youth Division were forced to retreat. When the officer in charge of the division was killed, Meyer was chosen to replace him. He was promoted from colonel to SS brigadeführer, which was equivalent to the rank of major-general in the Canadian Army. At the age of just 33, he was the youngest officer of his rank in the German armed forces.

His division was soundly defeated. By late summer, most members of the Hitler Youth Division had either been killed or captured. Meyer was making his way back to Germany, hoping to find more troops and organize a new division, when he was captured by partisans near Liege in southern Belgium. They turned him over to U.S. troops, who took him to a POW camp where he tried to hide his high rank and his SS affiliation.

He posed as a regular army colonel. For awhile he got away with the deception, but soon a fellow-prisoner gave him away and he was transferred to a prison camp for high-ranking Nazis in England. That's where he stayed until the war ended.

Meanwhile, Canadian Army investigators found plenty of proof to confirm that the POWs had been murdered by the Germans. French Resistance members had seen some of the shootings being carried out, and one of the former Canadian prisoners took war crimes investigators to the small church where Meyer's field headquarters had been, and showed them where to dig. There they found the bodies of some of the murdered Canadian prisoners.

The Army investigators pieced together the details of what had happened, and increasingly the evidence pointed toward Kurt Meyer, who was conveniently available for prosecution. The Army tried to establish a legal foundation for Meyer's prosecution.

There was no law which specifically covered war crimes, but several pieces of international jurisprudence applied. There was the Hague Convention, dating back to 1907, which said it was illegal to kill an enemy who had surrendered. And the Geneva Convention of 1929 said prisoners must be treated humanely.

The rules on how prisoners were to be treated were high-minded but were often broken by both German and Allied soldiers. In the dehumanizing chaos of battle, soldiers of both sides were guilty of mistreating POWs. Commanders knew this, and knew that unless officers in the field strictly enforced the rules, their troops would kill prisoners.

The Canadian authorities were determined to make sure that Meyer's prosecution did not smack of "victor's justice." Prime Minister Mackenzie King said that "the procedure will be in accordance with the principles of justice. . . . The proceedings will be conducted with dignity, fairness and justice."

Still, the regulations under which Meyer was tried permitted hearsay evidence to be admitted by the military court, and that cast a taint over the proceedings. There was also the fact that the five-member panel appointed to sit in judgment of Meyer consisted entirely of Army officers who had fought against him during the war. They could hardly be seen to be unbiased jurists.

On the other hand, Meyer simply could not be treated the same way as an alleged civilian murderer would be treated in a Canadian courtroom. What was the Army supposed to do – go out and round up a dozen Nazis to serve as jurors, so Meyer could be tried by a jury of his peers? Should he be let off the hook because the best potential witnesses – his own troops – would not or could not testify against him?

Following normal criminal procedure in military war crimes cases just wouldn't work. "It would," said chief prosecutor Bruce Macdonald, "in many cases be completely futile to attempt to convict admitted war criminals, and the guilty would escape just retribution."

And having gone to so much trouble to bring Meyer to trial, the Army was not about to let that happen. One way or another, the Army was determined to make sure that after a fair trial, Meyer would without doubt be found guilty.

CHAPTER 2

Death Sentence Commuted

Kurt Meyer's trial was held in December 1945 in Aurich, a small town in northern Germany. A naval barracks was converted into an ornate courtroom featuring dark oak panelling, chandeliers and a large Canadian Ensign flag fastened to the wall.

Meyer was marched into the courtroom by a major and a captain, chosen because they were members of regiments which had lost men taken prisoner by the murderous Nazi troops. Meyer looked more like a janitor than a general. He wore a plain German Army uniform, without his military decorations, symbols of rank or headgear, but the Army couldn't take away his military bearing, or his imposing physical presence.

He was five feet nine inches tall, broad-shouldered, thick-set and muscular. He wore his long, dark-brown hair combed back. He was flat-nosed, thick lipped, and had blue-grey eyes.

He made a slight bow to the five former battlefield opponents now sitting in judgment on him, then took his place in the prisoner's box. The chief judge was Major-General Harry Foster. Four brigadiers, one step below Foster in rank, flanked him.

The spectators were mainly Allied military personnel, but several German civilians had been brought in so "the German people" could hear about the crimes committed by one of their military leaders. One of these civilians was Kate Meyer, the accused man's wife and the mother of his five young children.

The charges were read out in English, then translated into French and German. Meyer faced five counts of committing war crimes. Specifically, he was said to have:

1) incited troops under his command to "deny quarter";

2) been "responsible for" the killing of 23 Canadian prisoners of war on June 7 [1944] near the villages of Buron and Authie in Normandy;

3) personally given orders to troops under his command to kill seven more prisoners at his headquarters at the old church, l'Ancienne Abbaye Ardenne, on June 8;

4) been "responsible for" the killing of the same seven prisoners. (This was an alternative wording for the third charge, in the event that there was insufficient proof that he gave orders for the killings);

5) been "responsible for" the killing of 11 other prisoners of war at his headquarters on June 7, the day before the seven prisoners mentioned in counts 3 and 4, were killed.

In summary, Meyer was being blamed for the murder of 41 unarmed Canadian soldiers.

Over the next two weeks, about 30 prosecution witnesses were called to prove the case. The Army was determined not only to have justice done, but to have everyone see that justice was being done.

The prosecution witnesses included former members of Meyer's regiment, who said they heard him say that his regiment was going to take no prisoners. The implication was that Meyer had hinted broadly that his soldiers should kill Allied prisoners, but didn't want to come right out and say it. This made him sound sneaky as well as sinister.

Other German witnesses described the young, excited and ruthless German soldiers who had been under Meyer's command. In basic training, these troops were said to have been told they were to take no prisoners. The implication was that everyone, including Meyer, knew about the take-no-prisoners policy. Still other ex-soldiers told the court that Meyer was a strict disciplinarian. This made it seem unlikely that Meyer's troops would have killed the Canadian POWs without his approval.

The most damaging witness was Jan Jesionek, a 19-year-old Pole who had been forced into the army and ended up in Meyer's regiment. Jesionek swore that he was at Meyer's Abbaye Ardenne headquarters on June 7, 1944, and heard him give the orders that resulted in the execution of the seven Canadian POWs.

Jesionek quoted Meyer as saying: "What should we do with these prisoners? They only eat up our rations."

Then, according to Jesionek, Meyer said: "In future, no more prisoners are to be taken."

Shortly after that, Jesionek testified, the seven prisoners were taken outside the church and shot.

The defence was flimsy. Meyer didn't even get to pick his own lawyer. He was represented by Maurice Andrew, a lieutenant-colonel in the Canadian Army who seemed resigned to the fact that his client would be convicted.

Andrew told the court that almost every witness Meyer had suggested be called was either "unavailable," or could not be found. Andrew called only one former member of Meyer's regiment. That witness recalled that when 150 enemy soldiers were taken prisoner on July 10, Meyer issued orders that they be put inside buildings to shelter them from a storm. The witness said this was typical of the humane way Meyer treated prisoners.

But the defence called no witnesses who could tell the court about the specific cases set out in the charges against Meyer. So it was left to the defendant himself to give his side of the story.

Meyer was calm on the stand, despite the fact that his life was on the line. He described the frantic battle which occurred in Normandy, and seemed to catch the judges' interest when he provided details of the tactics he had used against them on the battlefield.

Meyer flatly denied ordering the execution of prisoners, but had trouble explaining away incriminating statements he had made when war crimes investigators interrogated him in a British prison. Initially, Meyer denied any knowledge of Canadian POWs being found dead near his headquarters. Then, after he was told that he was going to be tried for the murder of those prisoners, he changed his story.

He admitted he had lied. He said he knew that some Canadian POWs had been killed by his men, but claimed he didn't find out about this until several days after the shootings. He acknowledged that he did not punish the soldiers who had committed these murders, suggesting that at least tacitly he approved of them.

He admitted that some of the shootings occurred less than 100 yards from his headquarters, but could offer no explanation as to why he had not heard the shots.

The trial ended just before Christmas. A couple of days later, Harry Foster announced the verdict.

The court found Meyer not guilty on the second and third counts, but guilty on the other three counts. He was held to be "responsible for" the murder of the seven prisoners at his headquarters on June 8, and also "responsible for" the killing of the 11 prisoners at his headquarters on June 7. He was also found guilty of inciting his troops to "deny quarter" to enemy soldiers.

Many years later, Foster told his son, Tony Foster, an author who was writing a book about the war, that he and the other judges felt Meyer had to take the blame for what his men had done.

"We agreed unanimously that he bore a vicarious responsibility for all the killings that took place at the Abbaye," Foster said. The general also revealed that the judges didn't believe Meyer when he denied knowing about the execution of the POWs near his headquarters.

"It was inconceivable," said Foster, "how he, sitting in his headquarters, could have heard a succession of regularly spaced pistol shots less than 150 feet away and not sent someone off to investigate. I would have, as would any commanding officer, particularly so close to the front. Meyer didn't. He didn't because he knew what was going on – even if he hadn't given the order."

Meyer had a chance to speak again before he was sentenced. He didn't dispute the fact that troops under his command killed the Canadian prisoners, but repeated his denial that he had ordered it or approved it. Then he threw himself on the mercy of the court.

"How far a commander can be held responsible for misdeeds of individual members of his troop," he said, "the soldiers of this court must decide."

The following day, Meyer stood stiffly at attention as his fate was announced: "The sentence of the court is that you suffer death by being shot," Foster said.

Meyer's jaw tightened. He flushed. He bowed to the judges. Then he was marched out of the courtroom.

Meyer had the right to appeal to the commander of the Canadian Army Occupation Forces, Major-General Chris Vokes. He did so, but on December 31 Vokes confirmed both the verdict and the sentence.

Vokes set no date for the execution, but Meyer knew it would be soon. He said goodbye to his family. A firing squad was appointed and rehearsed. The final order was issued. It said that Meyer was to be shot on January 4, 1946. But then the execution was delayed for three days to give British and U.S. intelligence officers a final opportunity to interrogate Meyer.

That brief delay saved Meyer's life. It provided Major-General Vokes with time to read over the record of the court proceedings more closely, and to reconsider Meyer's plea for mercy. Vokes decided to give Meyer a break.

He commuted the sentence to life in prison. When questioned by reporters about this, Vokes said he changed his mind because he didn't feel Meyer's "degree of responsibility" had been sufficiently established to warrant the death penalty. Later, he expanded on his reasoning:

> I concluded Meyer had been convicted on evidence that was sort of second-hand, and although he had a vicarious guilt, there was not a whit of evidence that he had given a direct order to have the soldiers executed.

There was a big pubic outcry in Canada when Vokes' decision to commute Meyer's sentence was announced. Letters and telegrams poured into Ottawa, and newspapers conjured up images of the dead Canadians lying in their graves, crying out in protest against the commuted death sentence. But the furor soon died down.

Meyer was transferred to a jail in England. A few months later, he was taken to Canada by ship and locked away in the federal penitentiary in Dorchester, New Brunswick. He was restless at first, but eventually became a model prisoner.

Most people soon forgot about Kurt Meyer, but he had a friend on the outside. German-born contractor Fred Lichtenberg, had immigrated to Canada in 1911, and lived in nearby Moncton. Lichtenberg, whose parents had known Meyer's family in the old country, started visiting Meyer in prison and sent money to Meyer's wife. Lichtenberg soon hired two Halifax lawyers to work for Meyer's release.

A public relations campaign was quietly started, seeking to present a sympathetic portrait of Kurt Meyer in jail. He was described as "cheerful" and never complaining. He was said to have a good sense of humor, and he was learning English. He was said to be a fine fellow, respected by his fellow-inmates and the warden.

Ralph Allen, a prominent journalist who had covered Meyer's trial, wrote an article in *Maclean's* magazine portraying Meyer as the victim of a kangaroo court. Allen said Meyer's legal rights had been violated at his trial, and the rules were bent to ensure a conviction.

In 1951, Meyer was transferred to a prison in Germany, ostensibly so he could be close to his family. The commander of the prison soon chopped Meyer's sentence from life to 14 years. With time off for good behavior, he got out of jail in 1954.

When he walked out the front gate, he got a hero's welcome from hundreds of Germans who had been following his case and pressing for his release. They cut tree branches to decorate the route from the prison to a nearby hotel, where a grand reception was held for the man whose imprisonment by the Canadians had turned him into a hero.

Meyer soon got a job as a salesman for a German brewery, trading on his fame to promote his company's products. He even wrote a book about his life. It was called *Panzergrenadiere*, and it made him even more of a celebrity. He became a popular advocate for Waffen SS veterans, trying to convince the public that the ex-soldiers were honorable German veterans, not Nazi war criminals.

Meyer died on December 21, 1961, his 51st birthday, and thousands of people attended his funeral. There were many tributes to the war hero known as "Panzer Meyer" throughout Germany. Nobody mentioned that he had been responsible for the murder of long-forgotten Canadian prisoners of war.

CHAPTER 3

"Just Following Orders"

Kurt Meyer wasn't the only ex-Nazi prosecuted by the Canadian military after the war. Six more were put on trial in 1946 for committing war crimes against members of the Royal Canadian Air Force.

Like Meyer, they were tried under rules which made the outcome of their trials virtually certain, so it wasn't surprising that they were all convicted. But unlike Meyer, none of them was of high rank, so they didn't get any breaks when it came to sentencing. Four of them were executed, and the other two got stiff prison sentences.

The first case involved a soldier named Johan Neitz who was accused of trying to kill an injured and unarmed RCAF officer. Flight Lieutenant Anthony Rudolph Roman had bailed out of a bomber which was shot down over Germany in 1944. Roman seriously injured his hip when he landed, and was soon taken into custody by the keeper of a nearby lighthouse.

The next day, Neitz arrived at the lighthouse to take Roman to jail. But the German army private decided to dole out a little punishment first. He forced the limping Canadian to pick up a 70-pound military flare and carry it as they set off towards town.

The two men walked for a while, then Roman stopped to rest, setting down the heavy flare. Neitz ordered him to pick it up and keep going. When Roman failed to respond, Neitz shot him. Other German soldiers arrived a few minutes later and took the seriously wounded Roman to a hospital.

After the war, Roman told war crimes investigators what had happened, and Neitz was charged with attempted murder. Roman was the chief witness against him. He testified that he didn't speak German, and didn't understand what Neitz was saying when he started waving his gun around.

Roman said that before he could respond to what appeared to be threats, Neitz fired at him twice, hitting him both times in the midsection.

Neitz's Canadian Army lawyer argued that the German was justified in using force because Roman had refused to obey his lawful order to pick up the flare. He claimed that Neitz's first shot was meant only to warn Roman, but his aim was off and the bullet inadvertently struck Roman.

Neitz, testifying in his own defence, said that Roman then made a motion with his hand, causing the German to believe the prisoner was reaching for a concealed weapon, so Neitz fired the second shot. He admitted that this time he meant to hit Roman, but said he only intended to wound him, not kill him. Therefore, he argued, he wasn't guilty of attempted murder.

The military court didn't buy Neitz's version of the events, especially since Neitz had previously searched Roman and knew the prisoner was unarmed.

Neitz was sentenced to life in prison.

The second trial involved another German soldier and a Nazi party official. They were charged with murdering an unidentified RCAF sergeant who, like Flight Lieutenant Roman, had bailed out over Germany after his bomber was hit by enemy fire. The sergeant was brought to the nearby town of Oberweier by German civilians.

Wilhelm Jung, who was the town's mayor and Nazi party leader, ordered two civilians to kill the Canadian prisoner. When they refused, Jung ordered a German soldier named Johann Georg Schumacher to do it. Schumacher took the Canadian prisoner outside the little town and shot him.

Lawyers for Jung and Schumacher maintained that there was a lot of confusion about what happened, and therefore the guilt of the accused men had not been proven beyond a reasonable doubt. But this weak defence fell apart after it was revealed that both Germans had made incriminating statements several months earlier, when they were questioned by Allied war crimes investigators.

If this had been a civilian trial, a key issue would have been whether those incriminating statements could be admitted as evidence at the trial. But the Canadian military officers who acted as judges in this case weren't concerned about legal technicalities. They permitted the incriminating statements to be introduced as evidence, and that sealed the fate of the two Germans.

Schumacher had admitted to war crimes investigators that he had shot the RCAF sergeant. "I refused at first," Schumacher told them, "but I was just a common soldier and must obey what my superiors ordered. As a common soldier I can't contradict my superior."

Schumacher admitted that he shot the Canadian airman twice, once in the head and once in the chest, then walked away, leaving the body lying in tall grass.

Jung also admitted his part in the crime. But like Schumacher, he tried to shift the blame to his superiors. Jung said that when he reported to his district leader that the Canadian sergeant had been captured, his leader had responded: "What, this air gangster still alive? Why hasn't he been beaten to death or shot?"

Jung said he took this as an order to kill the airman, and felt obliged to follow that order, but he didn't want to do the deed himself. So he told Schumacher to take the sergeant out and shoot him.

Jung said he started worrying about what would happen if the Allies won the war and found out about the killing, so he sent soldiers out to find the body and bury it. Later, he decided that this wasn't enough, so he had the Canadian's corpse dug up and his military identification tags removed before the body was reburied.

The court convicted both men. Under the broadly-worded military regulations in effect at the time, it was only necessary for the prosecution to show that Jung and Schumacher had been "concerned in the killing" of the RCAF sergeant. Since there was no doubt that they were "concerned in the killing," the inevitable verdict was guilty.

Jung and Schumacher paid for their war crimes with their lives. A few weeks after their trial, they were executed by a military firing squad.

Three more German soldiers were brought before a military court at Aurich in the third and final war crimes trial held by the RCAF. Their case was also based primarily on statements they had previously given to war crimes investigators.

The three Germans – Robert Holzer, Walter Weigel and Wilhelm Ossenbach – scrambled to put the blame for their crimes on others, but all three admitted taking some part in the killing of several Canadian airmen who had bailed out near Opladen, Germany.

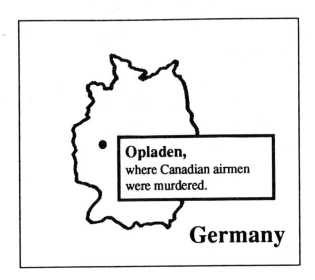

In one case, a captured flyer was severely beaten, then driven to a remote wooded area. He was half-dead when he arrived at the execution spot. Ossenbach coldly recalled what happened next.

"He was in such pain that I don't suppose that he cared what happened any more," Ossenbach said. Weigel and Holzer shot the prisoner, while Ossenbach stood and watched.

Both of the Germans who fired the shots came up with excuses for what they had done. "I drew my pistol with the firm intention not to shoot the pilot, but to shoot in a different direction," Weigel testified. Holzer claimed that he fired only after a superior officer threatened to shoot him if he didn't shoot the Canadian.

All three Germans tried to pin the blame for the murder on a mysterious Gestapo officer named Lieutenant Schaefer, who conveniently had eluded the Allies. The three men said they were just following Schaefer's orders.

The court ruled that even if there really was a Lieutenant Schaefer who had ordered them to kill the prisoner, it was an unlawful order and the three Germans should have refused to obey it.

"The killing of an innocent person can never have been justified," the court said. Rather than shoot the prisoner, the German soldiers should have refused to obey the order, the court said, even if that meant giving up their own lives.

All three men were convicted. Weigel and Holzer were executed by a firing squad. Ossenbach, the one who claimed he just watched, got off with 15 years in jail.

About 40 more war crimes investigations were under way when this trial was completed, but those cases were abandoned when the Canadian government decided in 1947 to withdraw its remaining Army and RCAF personnel from Europe.

The British Army picked up a few of the unfinished Canadian cases, but most of them were dropped when the British also decided to stop holding war crimes trials in 1948.

Before they took that step, the British informed the Canadian government of their intentions, and explained their position this way:

> In our view, punishment of war criminals is more a matter of discouraging future generations than of meting out retribution to every guilty individual. Moreover, in view of future developments in Germany envisaged by recent tripartite talks, we are convinced that it is now necessary to dispose of the past as soon as possible.

The British invited the Canadians to comment on the proposed end of war crimes prosecutions, and the Canadians replied that they had no comment to make. In this round-about way, Ottawa gave its quiet approval to the British decision to stop prosecuting Nazi war criminals.

And so, with the Canadian government's blessing, many Germans who would undoubtedly have been found guilty of committing war crimes against Canadian prisoners ended up getting off scot-free.

The Canadian government made no announcement about this, so the public didn't realize it had been done. The war criminals issue quietly slipped off the public agenda, but only for a while.

CHAPTER 4

The Missing General

Before they left Germany, Canadian Army investigators were itching to get their hands on at least one more Nazi war criminal. He was Wilhelm Mohnke, and if he had been put on trial after the war ended he almost certainly would have been executed.

But since the Canadians couldn't find him, they eventually concluded that Mohnke was dead. In fact, the Russians had grabbed him and locked him up in a Moscow prison, where he remained until 1955. By that point, Allied interest in prosecuting war criminals had vanished.

Mohnke was the colonel who commanded the Waffen SS regiment which fought beside Kurt Meyer's regiment in Normandy. Mohnke was said to have been even worse than Meyer. He was said to have personally given orders to gun down Canadian prisoners, and to have watched while some of those murders were committed.

After the war, German officers told war crimes investigators that Mohnke frequently ordered his troops to shoot captured enemy soldiers. Normandy was neither the first nor the last place where he was said to have done this.

Mohnke reportedly ordered the slaughter of 90 British POWs near Dunkirk in 1940, and was in command of troops who murdered 72 American POWs in the German Ardennes offensive in 1945.

Canadian Army investigators concluded that Mohnke was "at least indirectly responsible" for the killings of 35 Canadian prisoners at Fontenay-le-Pesnel in Normandy. This massacre, which occurred on June 8, 1944, is believed to be the worst crime ever perpetrated against members of the Canadian Armed Forces.

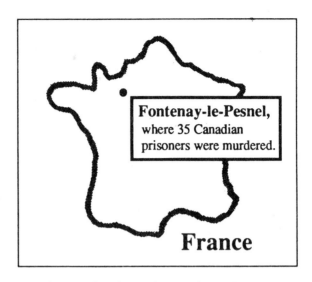

Fontenay-le-Pesnel, where 35 Canadian prisoners were murdered.

France

Mohnke was also said to have been "directly responsible" for at least three other murders in Normandy. According to Witold Stangenberg, a Polish motor mechanic who was drafted into the Waffen SS, Mohnke personally ordered the shooting of the three Canadians.

Stangenberg said he saw Mohnke and other officers questioning the prisoners for about 20 minutes in a field near Haut du Bosq. Then, according to Stangenberg, the Canadians were marched to the edge of a bomb crater. As Mohnke and the other officers looked on, the three prisoners were machine-gunned and their bodies fell into the crater.

After the war, Stangenberg led war crimes investigators to the spot. Identification tags from one of the prisoners were found in the bushes, and three badly decomposed bodies were recovered from the waterlogged crater.

Mohnke spent the final months of the war in Germany. He was promoted to SS brigadeführer (major-general) and put in command of the Reich chancellery in Berlin. As the Russians advanced, Mohnke was among the last to speak to Hitler before he committed suicide. Mohnke then ordered the bunker set on fire, and Hitler's body was burned beyond recognition.

Shortly afterwards, Mohnke was captured by the Russians and taken to Moscow, but the Russians didn't tell the Western Allies about this. They apparently wanted to pump Mohnke for information without sharing it with their former military partners.

The Canadians naively kept looking for Mohnke and put his name on CROWCASS, the Central Registry of War Criminals and Security Suspects. But Mohnke was one of some 85,000 suspects whose names were on the list, and he was all but forgotten in the post-war years, especially after the Canadian Army pulled out of Germany in 1947.

Mohnke spent 10 years in Moscow's Lubyanka prison before quietly returning to Germany in 1955. Again, the secretive Russians didn't share this information with their former allies, so Mohnke was able to quietly re-establish himself. He became a prosperous businessman in Hamburg.

But in the mid-1970s, his past started catching up with him.

The West Germans were still prosecuting war criminals, even though the war had been over for 30 years. Eventually they got around to Mohnke, but he denied the charges and without a confession, the Germans didn't feel they had a strong-enough case to take him to court.

Meanwhile, the Canadian government learned from a writer who was working on a book about the massacre of the British POWS at Dunkirk that Mohnke was living in West Germany. Ottawa offered to provide German prosecutors with the evidence against Mohnke collected by the Canadian Army after the war, but the Germans didn't respond, so the Canadians let the matter drop.

Ten years later, Mohnke's name came up again, this time before the Deschênes commission, which was looking into war criminals in Canada. William Douglas, a Department of National Defence historian, told the commission that the government wasn't concerned that its offer to help the West German prosecutors in the mid-1970s was ignored.

At that time, Douglas recalled, government policy was to take no action against suspected war criminals living in Canada. The government didn't want to stir things up by making a public fuss about the Germans' failure to prosecute Mohnke.

Bruce Macdonald, who was the chief prosecutor in the Kurt Meyer case, told the Deschênes commission of the Army's fruitless efforts to find Mohnke in the post-war years. The passage of four decades hadn't dulled Macdonald's desire to see Mohnke brought to justice.

"He is a person, if ever located, that ought to be prosecuted," Macdonald said. But the Deschênes commission wasn't interested in following up this old case. Its assignment was to look into war criminals currently in Canada, and the information about Mohnke wasn't germane to its task.

The Canadian news media, however, found the story interesting enough to pursue. Neil Macdonald, a reporter with the Ottawa Citizen, tracked down Mohnke in Germany. The old general said:

> A lot of soldiers were captured in Normandy. None, repeat none, were shot on my order. Do you understand? My men were disciplined, tough, and soldiers. . . . In war, it becomes very easy to kill someone. Human life becomes worthless. It takes discipline, hard discipline, to overcome that urge and fight to a goal. . . . I am a man of discipline. The SS was discipline. War is not some woman's job, you know.

The West Germans renewed their investigation of Mohnke in 1988. An investigator named Hartwig Negendank travelled to Ottawa and reviewed the old records, including the statement from the Polish mechanic who claimed to be an eyewitness to the shooting of the three Canadians near the bomb crater. But by that point, the mechanic was dead and the case was 44 years old. Negendank said he found nothing of use to his investigation, and didn't even bother to interview Mohnke.

"Why would I?" Negendank replied when asked about this by a reporter. "It would be a scandal if I were to go to him empty-handed and try to lure him into saying something."

Heinrich Wille, a public prosecutor in West Germany, provided further insight into the casual way the Germans were handling the Mohnke case.

Said Wille:

> According to our legal system there is no reason to speak to anyone if you don't have new information. We know about the crimes of the SS, but the problem is we don't know about the crimes of Mr. Mohnke. Maybe he was guilty. Maybe he was not.

It looked as if the case was closed, but it came up yet again. In 1989, a book was published with more details on what Mohnke allegedly had done. Titled *Hitler's Last General – The Case Against Wilhelm Mohnke*, the book described the massacre of the 35 Canadian servicemen after they surrendered to Mohnke's troops in

Normandy. Ian Sayer, one of the book's authors, called for action in the old case. "If Wilhelm Mohnke is not prosecuted on the evidence contained in this book," Sayer maintained, "then all war crimes trials wherever they may occur all over the world should be stopped immediately."

And yet, Mohnke was still not prosecuted. The Germans closed their file on the old general in 1993, saying there was insufficient evidence to keep it open. But still, the news media refused to let the Mohnke case drop. In 1994, American journalists took up the case.

An ABC television network program marking the 50th anniversary of D-Day claimed that Mohnke was debriefed by the U.S. Central Intelligence Agency upon his release from the Soviet prison in 1955. The program said Mohnke had provided information on fellow Nazis and SS veterans, in return for money and immunity from prosecution.

Reporters from British newspapers also got into the act. They interviewed a veteran of Dunkirk named Burt Evans who recalled that in 1940 he and other soldiers were taken prisoner by SS troops led by Mohnke, who was then only a captain.

Evans quoted Mohnke as saying, "You yellow English have come to the point of no return." Then, according to Evans, Mohnke pulled a hand grenade from his boot and threw it on the ground in front of the British prisoners, killing several of them and wounded others.

Charlie Daley, another British veteran who had been at Dunkirk, said SS men commanded by Mohnke opened fire on more than 80 prisoners with automatic weapons. Daley said he lost consciousness after he was covered with the bleeding bodies of his comrades.

More than half a century later, Daley said he was still tormented by nightmares about what had happened at Dunkirk. He said that no matter how old Mohnke and other war criminals were, they should be prosecuted.

"What they did was pure, premeditated evil," Daley concluded. "I am still suffering, and they should pay the price."

On the 50th anniversary of D-Day in June 1994, Mohnke was still alive. He was 83 years old, and somewhat of a celebrity, since he was the last former SS general living.

Journalists tried to interview him, but he refused to answer his phone or come to the door of his yellow-brick bungalow in a suburb of Hamburg. Neighbors said he was a pleasant old man who occasionally strolled down the street or worked in his garden.

CHAPTER 5

Forgive the Guilty?

Many of the immigrants who ended up in Canada after the war were East Europeans. Some had willingly served the Nazis as police officers, jailers, administrators and so forth, but a few of them were even worse.

They were cold-blooded murderers, anti-semites who happily took advantage of the invitation by the Nazis to persecute and kill Jews. These people were the worst war criminals in Canada. It is unfortunate they were let into the country. Their admission to Canada is not something the government set out to do. Looking back at the circumstances which prevailed at the time, it is possible to understand how it happened.

Ethnic animosities ran deep in Eastern Europe, and broke out into violence during the war. Jews were targeted by many of their fellow-countrymen, who eagerly did the Nazis' dirty work for them. Sometimes these people shocked even their SS officers by showing such enthusiasm for their grisly task. Anti-semitism went back for centuries, and was part of the dark side of East European culture.

After the tide of the war turned, the Nazis' henchmen joined the flow of refugees fleeing to the West. When these killers and collaborators slipped into their new roles, they looked and acted just like everyone else. Generally they got away with this deception, unless they happened to be recognized and denounced by some of their former victims.

Their success in blending in with their fellow-countrymen raised an interesting question: If they were so bad, why didn't they continue their criminal activities in the West? The obvious answer is that they were too smart for that. They knew they couldn't get away with their old behavior in a society which wouldn't tolerate it.

But an alternative theory offers a more interesting and controversial, answer. This theory maintains that war criminals made the transition to peacetime roles so easily because they weren't really criminals at heart. They didn't behave like criminals once they were free of the evil influence of the Nazis, and once they left the hate-filled environment of Eastern Europe behind them.

This might account for the fact that not only did they behave themselves in displaced persons camps in Western Europe, they also became decent and law-abiding citizens after they came to Canada.

According to this theory, these East Europeans were basically good by nature, but got caught up in the wickedness of their times. They reverted to their true and good natures once the powerful and corrupting Nazi influence was removed, and once they became part of the racially tolerant Canadian society.

It's a lot like the social worker's argument that there's no such thing as a bad boy. A kid might steal cars and mug people, but he does it because he comes from a bad home and has been led astray by bad companions. Put this boy in a decent environment, smother him with love and kisses, give him worthwhile goals, and he'll grow up to be a fine young man – or so the theory goes.

The suggestion that East European war criminals weren't really bad people has been supported by studies which show that almost anyone is capable of committing atrocities. Brainwash a man. Make him believe the people in positions of authority over him expect such behavior. Convince him to carry out orders. Show him that everyone else is doing it, and before long you can persuaded almost anyone to torture and kill people – or so some psychologists say.

Taking this theory a step further, you can even argue that the East European victimizers were actually victims themselves, good folks turned into monsters by the wicked Nazis operating in an anti-semitic environment. Therefore, war criminals can't be held accountable for their sins, because they weren't really to blame for their actions. They were victims of circumstances.

As the old saying goes, "The Devil made me do it." In more contemporary terms, they were good people caught up in an evil environment. When their environment changed, their actions changed. Therefore, to blame them for what they did in the past is unjust.

It's an interesting if dubious theory, but the victors and the victimized in post-war Europe certainly didn't see things that way. They thought war criminals were bad people who had done bad things, and they wanted to punish as many of them as possible for their hideous crimes.

But that turned out to be a huge and difficult task, far easier said than done. Inevitably, it ended up being carried out in an unfair and haphazard manner.

Essentially, it was a problem of magnitude. There were just too many of them, and they were spread over such a vast area that it was impossible to identify and round them all up.

It was much easier to single out the Germans, and particularly the ring-leaders, including the 21 top surviving Nazis who were put on trial by the Allies at Nuremberg in 1945-46, and the 177 lower-ranking Nazis – physicians, judges and so forth – who were brought before subsequent Nuremberg tribunals until 1949.

But the war produced tens of thousands of what might be called "hidden" war criminals. Most of them were East Europeans, and some of them ended up getting into Canada.

They were the ones who carried out much of the day-to-day work of the Holocaust, in which six million Jews were slaughtered. In addition, a great many gypsies, homosexuals, communists and others were killed, to say nothing of the many more who were raped, tortured, imprisoned and otherwise abused, but who managed to survive.

In total, it would be conservative to say that war crimes were committed against at least 12 million people. It took a lot of criminals to commit that many crimes.

Imagine trying to identify all these criminals. Imagine trying to round them all up and sort out them all out, particularly when their crimes were committed during the chaos of war, and were often carried out in secret.

The authorities tried their best to track down the war criminals, but it was a hopeless task, and a high percentage of them went unpunished.

Massive lists were compiled from Nazi records, interrogations, survivors' statements and other sources, but the lists eventually grew to contain thousands and thousands of names. Keeping track of all these people in those pre-computer days was an information-management nightmare.

And many war criminals "beat" the lists simply by changing their names. It was easy to do, especially when so many people didn't have passports, work records and other documents to confirm their identities.

The search for war criminals was further complicated by the fact that Eastern Europe had fallen under Soviet control. The Cold War was the best thing that could have happened to East European war criminals. Animosity between the East and the West made it hard for the Allies to examine records held by the uncooperative communists. It enabled war criminals to tell false stories which couldn't be checked by immigration officials from Canada and other countries.

Add to this the fact that chaotic conditions prevailed in post-war Europe, and so there were plenty of other things to worry about besides taking care of "old business." Europe's economy was shattered, food was scarce and displaced persons camps were overflowing. Pressure was strong to try and solve the many problems which currently existed, rather than dwelling on the past.

So finding and punishing war criminals wasn't a top priority, particularly after the anger against former enemies began to fade, and a new sense of cooperation began to emerge among those who were against the communists.

With those factors in mind, put yourself in the place of a Canadian immigration officer working in a displaced persons' camp in post-war Europe. Perhaps you can see how a war criminal might have gotten past you.

Suppose you're considering the case of a "refugee" from Eastern Europe who was part of a squad which killed Jews. He tells you a convincing story about how he worked as a farmer in his homeland until it was over-run by the Nazis, and then by the Soviets. He tells you how lucky he was to escape, and how he lost everything, including his identity papers.

He gives you a false name, which doesn't appear on any of the long lists of war criminals you're supposed to check, if you can wade through them all. A glance under his arms reveals no tell-tale tattoo indicating that he served in the SS.

He says he's unable to go home because the Soviets will execute him or send him to Siberia as a traitor, even though he has done nothing wrong. He tells you he hates the communists, which is in his favor, since your bosses have told you not to let communists into Canada.

Canadian farmers are crying for labor, and he says he wants to work on a farm in Canada. He's a member of an ethnic group which has a large number of people already living in Canada. One of them has offered to sponsor him and guarantee that he won't become a drain on the public purse.

All things considered, would you have let this man into Canada? You probably would, and that's how an undetermined number of East European war criminals got into Canada.

That's not to say that all the war criminals who beat the screening system were clever liars who fooled immigration officers. Sometimes they apparently were deliberately let in, even though the immigration department had good reason to believe they were war criminals. These cases are more disturbing, because they suggest that government officials deliberately approved applications which should have rejected.

Consider the example presented by Ethyl Ostry, a Canadian nurse who worked in Germany after the war. Ostry was employed in a sanatorium for displaced persons who were under United Nations care. She recorded her observations in her diary which eventually ended up in Ottawa as part of the material examined by the Deschênes commission.

Ostry wrote:

> The DP patients who were aware among themselves which ones were collaborators regarded with ironic humour the laxity of the screening process. But the result was no joke. Groups of patients who were known as hardened Nazis were confirmed in their DP status and took advantage of having passed the test to harass and even steal from other patients.

Ostry said that when Canadian immigration teams came to the sanatorium to recruit labor for various industries in 1947, they tried hard to weed out communists, but didn't seem to care about people with fascist backgrounds.

"I was shocked," Ostry wrote,

> to find that one of the women working in Gauting Sanatorium, well known for her past Nazi activities, who had been screened out as a collaborator by the American military team and lost her DP status, but remained employed under the status of German personnel, was accepted for resettlement in Canada.

As required, she signed a contract to work as a domestic at the rate of $35 a month for a year, at the end of which time she could if she chose enter other employment.

I pointed out to the Canadian immigration representative the fact that the woman had been deprived of her DP status and asked how she could be considered eligible for resettlement in Canada. In spite of this, the woman gaily announced to me a few days later that she was about to leave for Canada.

How many other cases of this nature occurred will never be known, but Ostry's comment that immigration teams "didn't seem to care about people with fascist backgrounds" suggests that this was not an isolated case.

Early Cases

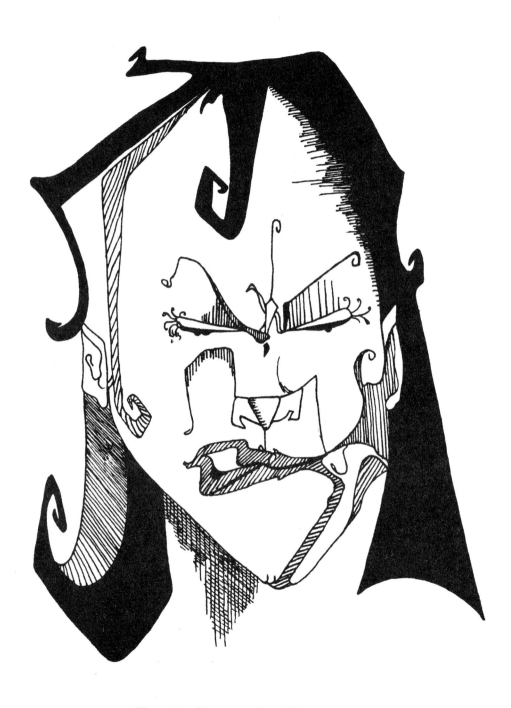

Hermine Braunsteiner Ryan

CHAPTER 6

The Criminal Count

Jacques de Bernonville is the first war criminal known to have come to Canada in a bid to escape justice. He snuck into the country in 1947, and once his presence became know there was a big outcry of protest.

But he also got a lot of public support, particularly in Quebec, and this helped him stay in Canada for several years before he was finally given the boot.

Jacques de Bernonville collaborated with the Nazis when they occupied his native France. He helped the Germans round up Jews and tortured members of the French resistance movement who fought bravely against the Nazis.

After the war, de Bernonville managed to make it to the United States, and from there he slipped across the border into Quebec, using a phony passport and dressed as a priest.

Quebec was a good hiding place for him because he could easily blend into the French-Canadian population. It was also an ocean away from France, and the further away the better as far as de Bernonville was concerned. The French government was prosecuting traitors like him, and if his fellow-countrymen had gotten their hands on him, they would likely have executed him.

He managed to find people in Quebec with pro-Nazi sympathies who were willing to help him. These Quebecers didn't consider the things that de Bernonville had done during the war to be crimes.

Rather, they saw him as an admirable figure who had fought bravely for what had turned out to be the losing side in the war.

They viewed him as a political refugee fleeing from the communists and socialists who had taken control of post-war France, and they did what they could to help him.

The man himself claimed not only to be a patriot, but also a French aristocrat. He said he could trace his lineage back to the French monarchy, and he grandly called himself Count Jacques Charles Noel Duge de Bernonville. His polished speech and suave manner helped make the claim believable.

He became an army officer when he was only 17, and fought against the Germans in the First World War, winning the Croix de Guerre for bravery. But after the war he his political views swung to the right and he became disillusioned with the liberal way things were going in his country.

In the 1930s he took part in street battles against French communists and smuggled arms from Italy into France in a bid to bring down the government and establish a right-wing regime. He also became an anti-semite, smashing the windows of Jewish shops.

When the Second World War broke out in 1939, de Bernonville once again fought for his country against the Germans, but after the Nazis took control of France in 1940 his right-wing political sympathies led him to become a traitor and work for the Germans. He became a Nazi agent in French North Africa, then came home to serve as a senior official in the puppet government established by the Nazis.

This government was led by a retired field marshal named Phillipe Petain, a First World War hero with fascist sympathies. Petain tried to pass himself off as a patriot, but in fact he was a puppet, and the Nazis pulled his strings.

Petain's headquarters were in Vichy in central France, so the collaborationist government became known as the Vichy regime. A significant number of people in Quebec were in sympathy with the Vichy regime, even though Canada was at war with the Germans. These people considered the quisling Petain to be the legitimate leader of France. So, after the war, these people didn't view de Bernonville as a criminal.

To them, he was an admirable figure and a man to be helped. But to most English Canadians, and to some French-Canadians, de Bernonville was a traitor and a war criminal.

During the war, de Bernonville served the Nazis as director of public order for the district of Lyon. He was also the commander of a pro-Nazi military group known as the Malice. It consisted of about 500 local men who helped the Germans round up members of the French resistance, captured Allied military personnel when they parachuted into France and helped the Nazis load Jews on trains bound for death camps.

Klaus Barbie, the German SS officer in charge of Lyon during the Nazi occupation, worked closely with de Bernonville. Barbie was eventually tracked down in South America in the 1980s, returned to France and jailed for his war crimes.

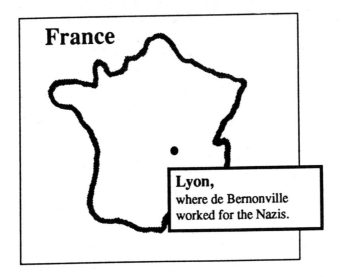

France

Lyon,
where de Bernonville worked for the Nazis.

After the Allies invaded France in 1944 and it became clear that the Vichy regime was going to fall, de Bernonville went into hiding in a Benedictine monastery. Eventually he made his way to Canada, where sympathetic French-Canadians provided him with a hiding place near Quebec City.

Meanwhile, he was tried *in absentia* by a French court. He was found guilty of committing treason, holding civilians hostage, ordering mass arrests, torturing resistance fighters and handing them over to the Gestapo for execution.

He was sentenced to death in 1947, but French authorities at the time were unaware he was hiding in Canada, and he went unpunished.

Meanwhile, de Bernonville started working for a powdered milk company in Granby, Quebec. He used a false name, but it didn't take long for his identity to be discovered. His high rank in the

Malice and his unsavory reputation among his fellow-countrymen made him a well-known figure. He was spotted by a former French resistance member who had emigrated to Canada, and his cover was blown.

The federal government quickly determined that de Bernonville had entered Canada with a false passport. That was grounds for deportation, but de Bernonville shrewdly came up with a way to avoid being sent back to France.

He claimed refugee status, which enabled him to remain in Canada while he fought in court against the deportation order. He painted himself as an honorable man unjustly accused of war crimes by his communist enemies in France. Some Quebecers sympathetic to him supported his claim for refugee status.

The case turned into another chapter in the continuing conflict between the French and the English in Canada, and de Bernonville became the centre of a political as well as a legal battle. The case dragged through the courts for three years as de Bernonville continued to enjoy his freedom.

Some high-level French-Canadians came out in support of de Bernonville, making it politically difficult for the government to kick him out of the country. Camillien Houde was one of his biggest backers.

Houde was a prominent French-Canadian nationalist who had opposed Canadian entry into the war so vigorously that he had been put in jail. He had openly advised French-Canadians to defy the government and refuse to submit to the military draft.

After the war, Houde was so popular among French-Canadians that he was elected mayor of Montreal and also a Member of Parliament. He soon tried to form a new political party and used de Bernonville to try and make the federal government look anti-Catholic and anti-French.

Other Quebec MPs and the Union Nationale government of Maurice Duplessis also supported de Bernonville. Robert Rumilly, a close political ally of Duplessis, acted as chief propagandist for the de Bernonville support campaign. In 1949, Rumilly gave a speech in which he tried to turn de Bernonville into a political martyr.

Rumilly claimed that "a shifty-eyed Jew" had invented "the most incredible calumnies about the noble commander de Bernonville." He went on to describe de Bernonville as a "legendary hero" and accused Ottawa of trying to "send him to his execution."

But not all French-Canadians backed de Bernonville. Veterans of General Charles de Gaulle's Free French forces who were living in Quebec publicized the crimes which de Bernonville and other Vichy collaborators had committed.

Meanwhile, a CCF Member of Parliament from Winnipeg named Alistair Stewart told the House of Commons that de Bernonville was a war criminal. Stewart quoted a French resistance fighter who recalled that:

> de Bernonville commanded my torturers to use electricity on me. They took a wire, which they spliced, attaching half to my handcuffs and pricking me with the other half, thus causing burns to my right arm and to the entire right side of my body and to my legs.

According to Stewart, de Bernonville's sadistic men then handed the resistance leader over to the Gestapo, which sent him to the Buchenwald concentration camp.

The federal government, headed by Louis St. Laurent, was caught in the middle. St. Laurent didn't want to help a convicted war criminal or give the impression that Canada welcomed such people, but he also didn't want to appear to be siding with the English-Canadians against a man who had a lot of French-Canadian support.

The Prime Minister feared a political backlash in Quebec if he authorized the deportation of de Bernonville to France. But eventually, after all the details of what de Bernonville had done during the war came to public light, the government was left with no choice but to send him packing.

To do otherwise would have been to openly admit that Canada was a haven for war criminals, and the authorities in Ottawa weren't willing to go that far to appease de Bernonville's supporters.

The minister of immigration gave de Bernonville 60 days to leave Canada, but helpfully told him he could go to any country that he chose, so long as he left Canada.

It was a way of booting de Bernonville out of Canada without sending him back to France. St. Laurent's private secretary, Pierre Asselin, even sent a letter to de Bernonville advising him to find a friendly country to go to.

The fast-fading de Bernonville took Asselin's advice, and in August 1951 he left for Brazil, where he remained for the next two decades. But ultimately, de Bernonville came to an unhappy end.

He was found strangled in his Rio de Janiero apartment in 1972, with a gag in his mouth and his hands and feet bound.

The Brazilian authorities said a servant had killed him, but some people didn't believe that. They claimed that de Bernonville was murdered by members of the Nazi network in South America.

In death, as in life, Jacques de Bernonville was controversial.

CHAPTER 7

The Ukrainian Patriots

About 2,000 soldiers who fought for the Nazis were permitted to come to Canada.

Whether they were war criminal or not was hotly debated at the time. Jewish groups claimed they had committed atrocities but their guilt was never proven, and after a long debate they were accepted as immigrants in the early 1950s.

These ex-soldiers were Ukrainians. They were members of the Galicia Division, which fought for the Germans against the Soviets. The Galicians were never in battle against Canadian or other Allied forces.

They were admitted to Canada despite the fact that they had been part of the SS, the Nazis' most fanatical organization. The Allied War Crimes Tribunal at Nuremberg denounced the SS as a "criminal organization." On that basis alone, the authorities in Ottawa could have turned the Galicians away.

But influential Ukrainian-Canadians convinced the government that their fellow-countrymen were honorable ex-soldiers and political refugees, not war criminals.

The Ukrainian-Canadians, a powerful political force, persuaded Ottawa that the Galicians were anti-communist nationalists and patriots who fought for the Germans not because they were pro-Nazis but because they were anti-communist.

But Canadian Jews, also a potent political group, blamed the Galicians for the persecution of Jews during the Holocaust and suggested that even if they were not collectively guilty, many individual members of the division had committed war crimes.

The Jews weren't the only ones speaking out against the Galicians. Not surprisingly, the Soviets also claimed the division was filled with cut-throats and killers. The Soviets demanded that the Galicians be returned to Ukraine so they could be punished for their alleged war crimes. But these communist demands were counter-productive, and helped convince Ottawa to admit the Ukrainians to save them from Soviet punishment.

Galicia,
where an SS division
was formed.

Ukraine

The Galician Division was sometimes called the Halychyna Division. Both titles were derived from names given to the part of the western Ukraine where most of the division's members came from. Galicia, like much of Eastern Europe, was taken over by the Soviets in 1939 after Hitler and Stalin made a deal to carve up the area between them.

Two years later, when the Germans turned on their Soviet allies and invaded Ukraine, they quickly drove out the Soviets and started rounding up Jews. They got plenty of help from the local population.

Anti-semitism was strong in Ukraine, and nationalists resented the fact that many Jews had supported the Russians. These Ukrainians eagerly joined the Nazis in going after the Jews.

The Germans got more help from the Ukrainians in 1943 when the Soviets started advancing. They persuaded the Ukrainians that the best way to fight the Russians was to fight for the Germans, and they set up the Galicia Division. The Ukrainians got to join their own military unit, and the Nazis got a fighting force which was more motivated and effective than an army of draftees would have been.

Turning the Ukrainians into soldiers and allies was a desperation move for the Nazis. Previously, when they had been winning the war, the Nazis had proclaimed that the Ukrainians and other Slavs were an inferior group, little better than Jews.

But when they needed the help of the Ukrainians to fight the Russians, the Germans changed their tune and treated the Ukrainians with respect, telling them they were a proud and noble people who should help the Nazis drive back the bolsheviks.

When the call went out for volunteers, the Ukrainians responded eagerly, especially after the Nazis said the Galician Division would have its own troop colors and insignia as well as its own chaplains. Ukrainian national leaders threw their support behind the new division, believing that eventually it would form the nucleus of a Ukrainian national army.

The Galicians were thrown into the fight in early 1944 about 50 miles east of the Galician capital of Lvov. The Ukrainians suffered heavy casualties against the better-armed, more-mechanized Russians.

Only about 3,000 of the division's 13,000 members remained alive and fit for duty when the Battle of Brody ended, but the unit was soon brought back up to strength with new blood. There was no shortage of Ukrainians who wanted to serve.

The rebuilt Galicia Division fought against the Russians in Slovakia and Yugoslavia, then retreated into Austria where the division's commanders, eager to avoid being taken by the Russians, surrendered to the British in May 1945.

The Ukrainian soldiers were initially sent to a prison camp in Rimini, Italy, where they underwent preliminary screening to determine whether they should be held on war crimes charges.

Nothing incriminatory was found, so the Allies proposed to repatriate them to their homeland. But the Galicians refused to return to Ukraine, which had by that point been taken over by the Russians. The ex-soldiers knew that if they went home the Russians would punish them for supporting the Nazis.

The Galicians appealed to Western countries for political asylum. They got a sympathetic response from the British, who

believed the Galicians weren't Nazis at heart. In 1947, D. Haldane
Porter, who headed the British Refugee Screening Commission,
went to the camp in Italy where the Galicians were being held.

"The general impression which we have formed of all the men
in the camp is favorable," Porter said in a report to the British
government,

> as they strike us all as being decent, simple-minded sort of
> people. The national emblem of the Ukraine, in the form of a
> trident, is freely displayed all over the camp, and the inmates
> clearly regard themselves as a homogeneous unit, unconnected
> either with Russia or Poland, and do not seem conscious of
> having done any wrong. . . .
>
> They probably were not, and certainly do not now seem to be
> at heart pro-German, and the fact that they did give aid and
> comfort to the Germans can fairly be considered to have been
> incidental and not fundamental.

The Galicians were soon transferred to England and put to work
on British farms. They replaced German prisoners of war who had
done the farm work in earlier years, but had been sent back to
Germany at the end of the war.

But the stay of the Galicians in Britain was a temporary measure. Eventually, the British government intended to give the farm
jobs to its own demobilized servicemen, so Canada and the other
dominions were asked to take some of the Galicians as immigrants.

Since Canada was looking for people to work in its booming
agricultural and natural resources industries, it was willing to
consider the idea, even though the Galicians bore the stigma of the
SS.

Thanks mainly to the lobbying efforts of the Ukrainian-Canadian community, the government was eventually persuaded to
accept about 2,000 of the Galicians as immigrants. Most Ukrainian-Canadians hated the communists and admired the Galicians
for having fought against the Russians. They viewed the Galician
soldiers as freedom fighters, not as war criminals.

Despite strong pressure from the Ukrainian-Canadians, the
government took about two years before deciding to accept the
Galicians. This was primarily because Jewish groups were so vocal
in their opposition to the Galicians.

The Jews claimed the Galicians had played a big part in the
Holocaust. Samuel Bronfman, president of the Canadian Jewish
Congress, said each member of the division "ought to be stamped
with the stigmata that is attached to the entire body of the SS."

The Jews insisted that the division helped the Nazis destroy the Polish ghetto in Warsaw. The Jews also claimed that many members of the division were fascists who committed atrocities against Jews before they joined the SS.

The Canadian Jews maintained that the Galicians had rounded up Eastern European Jews and sent them to slave labor camps, shot men in a town square, and locked women and children in a church and set the building on fire. They said some members of the Galician Division had worked as concentration camp guards.

But the Canadian Jews were unable to substantiate these claims, despite the fact that they put out a worldwide call for witnesses to come forward. After that, the wind went out of the Jewish activists' sails, and Canadian immigration officials went to Britain to screen applicants.

The Galicians soon started arriving. They got a lot of help from the Ukrainian-Canadian community, and quickly established themselves. As a group, they were model citizens who made a valuable contribution to the growth and development of their adopted land.

But the old charges against them kept popping up from time to time, and they were forced to go over the same old ground, denying repeatedly that what they had done for the Nazis made them war criminals.

CHAPTER 8

The Lucky Latvian

Haralds Puntulis was a lucky man.

While many of his fellow Latvians perished in the Second World War, he survived. Then he was fortunate enough to get out of Latvia before the communists took over, and thereby probably saved his life again.

The Soviets considered Puntulis to be a war criminal. If they'd been able to try and convict him they would likely have put him in front of a firing squad.

The fortunate Puntulis spent the early post-war years in a refugee camp in Sweden. It was crowded and dirty, but he got lucky again and managed to be accepted by Canada as an immigrant. After that, he was home free.

He lived a good life in Canada and died in peace, despite the fact that the communists and Canadian Jews kept saying he murdered thousands of Latvian Jews and gypsies during the war.

Puntulis repeatedly denied these charges, and during the 34 years he lived in Canada the government took no legal action against him.

Again, luck was with him. He lived at a time when the government had no interest in bringing suspected war criminals in Canada to justice. He also had the good fortune of being from Latvia, one of the Baltic states which was forcefully incorporated into the Soviet Union.

Although the Soviets asked the Canadian government to send him back to Latvia, Ottawa refused. The official reason was that there was no extradition treaty between Canada and the Soviet Union. But in fact, the government didn't want to send Puntulis home because he wouldn't get a fair trial in Latvia.

So Ottawa left Puntulis alone, even though two men who worked with him during the war were being prosecuted as war criminals in West Germany and the United States. In that sense, Puntulis was lucky again.

It wasn't until the mid-1980s that the Canadian government finally started prosecuting suspected war criminals, and by that point Puntulis ended up being lucky once more, if that's what you can call it. By the time the government was ready to go after him, he was dead.

He immigrated to Canada in 1948. As far as can be determined, he wasn't asked by immigration officials about links he might have had to the Nazis during the war. Such questions were not routinely asked of prospective East European immigrants at that time.

Puntulis undoubtedly *was* asked whether or not he was a communist. That was a question put to every prospective immigrant to Canada in the late 1940s, and on that score Puntulis was happy to tell the truth. He was certainly not a communist.

In fact, he turned out to be a splendid capitalist. He settled in Toronto area and quickly took advantage of the economic opportunities which were available to him. The city was booming, and Puntulis built a successful one-man business as a building contractor.

He oversaw construction projects and hired tradesmen to handle various parts of the work. He did a lot of home renovations, and built a nice house for himself and his wife Anna in Willowdale, a suburb north of Toronto. It was lovely red-brick place with a double garage, backing onto a park.

Unlike many other suspected war criminals who lived in anonymity after coming to Canada, Puntulis got a lot of public attention. It began when he was tried *in absentia* by a Soviet court in Latvia in 1965. The 19-day trial was covered by the CBC, so the case got plenty of publicity in this country.

He was convicted and sentenced to be shot, but that didn't mean a thing to Puntulis because he was safe in Canada. The Soviets had no way of getting their hands on him.

He kept working at his contracting business, and told friends and neighbors how fortunate he was to live in a free country instead of behind the Iron Curtain, where they trumped up phony war crimes charges against innocent people like himself.

Over the years, Puntulis was dogged by continuing allegations by the Soviets and members of the Canadian Jewish community. He was in the news again in the late 1970s when Jewish protesters demonstrated on his street, demanding that he be punished.

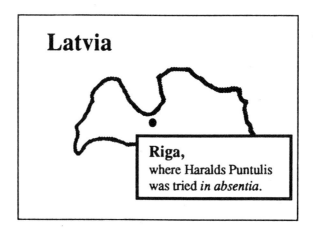

In 1982, just as the authorities in Ottawa were finally starting to look into the possibility of taking action against suspected war criminals in Canada, Puntulis died peacefully at his home at the age of 73.

Puntulis was gone, but the war crimes allegations against him lived on. A couple of months after his death, a magazine called *Today* carried an article about Puntulis. *Today* was distributed with the Saturday editions of several big newspapers.

The cover story of the August 28, 1982, issue was about Puntulis. It featured a black cover with a big swastika. The dramatic headline said, "War criminals in Canada: The issue that won't go away."

One of the main reasons why the war criminals issue wouldn't go away was that publications like *Today* wouldn't let it go away. They kept bringing it up, knowing that stories about alleged war criminals were interesting to readers, and sensing that government policy on the matter could be influenced.

Journalists who wrote such articles sometimes felt that publicizing the fact that war criminals were living in Canada would help put pressure on the government to do something about the problem. It was an example of what is known as "advocacy journalism."

Reporters Jeff Ansell and Paul Appleby were researching the story when Puntulis died. The article, which came out eight weeks later, made a strong case against him. (Puntulis's death freed the magazine from the danger of a libel suit.)

The story featured a graphic showing Puntulis's signature on the deed to his house in Willowdale, along with a Latvian police identity card bearing his name and signature. The article pointed out that the signatures matched. The identity card was issued by a rural police force known as the Aizsargi, which was noted for its anti-semitic wartime activities.

The story said Puntulis was working as a platoon commander in the Aizsargi police when the Nazis took over Latvia in 1941. The article portrayed him as eager to collaborate with the Germans, who promoted him to chief of police of the 4th precinct of the Rezekne district in the southeast part of the country.

That summer, Puntulis and his men were said to have killed all the Jews in three communities. Puntulis was said to have directed a firing squad in another town, lining up the victims in two ranks so that each victim could be shot twice, once in the head and once in the heart. Puntulis was also said to have personally gone along the ranks and fired a third shot into anyone who was still alive.

This and other evidence was originally presented against Puntulis at his trial in Latvia in 1965. It was a show trial, staged for propaganda purposes, featuring bright lights, movie cameras, an elevated stage and machine-gun-toting soldiers. Three empty chairs represented Puntulis and two other suspects who were not in court.

Collectively, Puntulis and five others were accused of having been responsible for the deaths of 5,128 Jews and 311 gypsies, as well as sending about 5,000 non-Jews to Germany as slave laborers. The trial featured confessions from the three accused men who were present, along with plenty of dramatic evidence from witnesses who said they had seen it all happen.

The CBC's Moscow correspondent, David Levy, covered Puntulis's trial. Levy was quoted in the *Today* article as telling his CBC audience in 1965:

> There is no doubt in my mind that the atrocities and massacres were committed. . . . I couldn't attempt here to report the grisly details. Let me just say that never in my life until then had I

actually heard a man calmly tell how on one of countless massacre assignments, he had flubbed the job of shooting an 11-year-old Jewish boy, and how his chief finished the boy off with a bullet in the head. That chief, by the way, was named as the one living in Canada.

That last sentence was a reference to Puntulis, whom Levy didn't name because of the danger that Puntulius would bring a libel action against CBC.

One of the other accused war criminals who was tried *in absentia* in Latvia in 1965 was Albert Eichelis. Fifteen years later, Eichelis was brought before a court in West Germany, where he had gone to live after the war.

Puntulis was called to testify in that case, but he didn't have to go to West Germany. He appeared before an Ontario Supreme Court examiner to give his testimony against Eichelis, who was Puntulis's boss during the war. Puntulis's evidence in the Eichelis case was forwarded to the West German court, but his testimony was kept secret.

The third empty chair at the 1965 trial in Latvia belonged to Boleslaus Maikovskis. He immigrated to the United States after the war. In the early 1980s, Maikovskis was prosecuted as a war criminal by the United States Justice Department, and Puntulis was interviewed in Toronto by a U.S. Justice Department lawyer in that case.

What he said there was also not made public. But a videotaped statement taken in Latvia in 1981 in connection with the Maikovskis case incriminated Puntulis.

On that videotape, a former Latvian police officer named Yazep Antonovich talked about what he and others had done while they were assigned to a police unit commanded by Puntulis. Antonovich described what was done to the Jews, on Puntulis's orders:

> They were shot with their faces toward the pit, and their clothes had been taken off. They were only in their underwear. . . . They fell into the pit. . . . There were horrible noises, cries, shouting. . . . I saw Maikovskis. I saw Puntulis. . . .

It was compelling testimony, and when it was printed as part of the article in *Today* magazine in 1982, it certainly made it seem as if Puntulis was guilty of war crimes.

But the article also quoted people who had good things to say about Puntulis. They were his friends and neighbors in

Willowdale, and they said they didn't believe he was a war criminal.

"He was cleared in this country by everybody and their brother," one neighbor said. "Let's everybody forget and go on. We've got more problems than that."

Another neighbor had a similar view. He said:

> We find both Harry and his wife extremely good citizens, and the whole neighborhood is very fond of them. We find it very difficult to believe that he's been involved in anything this horrendous. I know he worked for the forestry commission over there. That's what he did for most of the war – he was a forester.

Puntulis's denial of guilt was also accepted by the person who knew him best, his wife Anna. In the *Today* article, she was quoted as saying:

> Do you really think that I could ever live with a man that has done what Harry was accused of? I was with him through it, and he's never been involved in any of this.

CHAPTER 9

"Politically Notorious"

Six months after the end of the war, immigration officers were warned to watch out for Slovakian exiles trying to get into Canada.

"Should the politically notorious adherents to the pro-Nazi Tiso regime now in Austria apply for entry to Canada, they should be refused a visa," an Immigration Department bulletin said.

Yet by the early 1950s, 1,500 Slovakian exiles had been admitted to Canada, including several top officials of the "politically notorious" Tiso regime. How they got into the country is an interesting story, with elements of mystery and intrigue.

Named after its leader, a Roman Catholic priest named Joseph Tiso, the infamous Tiso regime didn't just co-operate with the Germans. It climbed right into bed with them, shamelessly collaborating with the Nazis in exchange for political power.

This "deal with the devil" helped the Slovakians achieve their nationalistic ambitions, at least nominally. It enabled them to separate from the Czechs, who had dominated them in the former country known as Czechoslovakia. The sovereign state of Slovakia was proclaimed on March 14, 1939. Independent in name only, it was a puppet of the Nazis.

The deal also eventually led to the annihilation of 70,000 of Slovakia's 90,000 Jews, who were rounded up by their fellow-countrymen and shipped off to death camps in Poland. But this atrocity was quickly forgotten by the Canadian government in the post-war years.

Slovakia

Bratislava,
where the Tiso regime
had its capital.

Ottawa, which initially was determined to keep adherents of the Tiso regime out of Canada, soon succumbed to pressure to let them in. That pressure came from several sources, most notably the 29,000-member Slovakian-Canadian community.

These people were eager to help their fellow-countrymen. They were well organized, and lobbied hard for the admission of the exiles. They offered to provide jobs for the newcomers and guaranteed that they wouldn't become a financial burden on Canadian taxpayers.

The Slovakian immigrants – like the Galicians from Ukraine – also got into Canada because they were on the right side in the Cold War. The exiles were staunchly anti-communist. This was a big advantage in the late 1940s and early 1950s, when the "red menace" was seen as the major threat to Canadian security. Canada was looking for anti-communist immigrants to offset left-wingers in various ethnic communities. The Slovakians, who by and large favored democracy or fascism, fit the bill nicely.

Not all the exiles had willingly backed the Tiso regime. Many of them were primarily patriots. They had supported Tiso only as a means to an end – which was to achieve national independence. The Slovakians were distinct from the Czechs in several ways, most notably in language, culture and religion. Their heritage stretched back for 1,100 years, and they resented being forced to live in Czechoslovakia, a country which had been created by the victors at the end of the First World War after the collapse of the Hapsburg empire.

There is evidence that at least some of the Slovakians were secretly resettled in Canada by Allied intelligence agencies, which used ex-Nazi collaborators as anti-communist agents in the early post-war years. New identities and new homes in Canada were said to have been a payoff to these Slovakians for their help in the fight against the Soviets and their allies, including the communists who took power in post-war Czechoslovakia.

Whether these claims are true or not remains to be seen. Ottawa has refused repeated requests from Canadian journalists and others to open secret files which could shed light on this matter. Access to Information Act requests have resulted in the release of small bits of information, together with long sections of files which have been blanked out, ostensibly for security reasons.

With the disintegration of the Soviet Union and the fall of communism in Europe, it's hard to see why Ottawa is still refusing to make this information public, unless it is to protect the government from political embarrassment for the faults committed by its predecessors.

Some of the Slovakian exiles were also said to have gotten into Canada with the help of the Roman Catholic Church. Slovakia was a devoutly Catholic country, and several intellectuals who were prominent in wartime Slovakia were able to get teaching positions in Catholic universities in Quebec.

There's no doubt that at least one prominent Slovakian exile had the active support of the Catholic Church. He was Karol Sidor, the organizer and first commander of the Hlinka Guard. This was the paramilitary arm of the Hlinka Party, named for its founder, Andrej Hlinka. After Hlinka's death in 1938, Joseph Tiso took over leadership of the party.

Sidor served briefly as Tiso's top official, but his reluctance to knuckle under to the Nazis led to his ouster in 1940. Sidor was dispatched to Rome as Slovakia's ambassador to the Vatican, a position he held until the end of the war. He couldn't go back to Czechoslovakia after the war, so he remained as an exile in the Vatican.

In the late 1940s, Pope Pius XII asked Canada to accept Sidor, and Prime Minister Louis St. Laurent agreed. He quietly ordered Immigration Department officials to waive the rules and admit Sidor, who died in 1953.

Several other prominent members of the Tiso regime also got into Canada. They included Karol Murin, former political secretary to Tiso; Matus Cermak, Slovakia's ambassador to Nazi Germany; Konstantin Culen, who served as propaganda minister; and Ferdinand Durcansky, foreign minister until he was purged by the Nazis; none of the above were brought up on charges of war crimes.

And then there was Joseph Kirschbaum, who was a protegé of Durcansky's and one of the most interesting Slovakians who ended up in Canada. Many years after his arrival, his past came back to haunt him.

Kirschbaum was born in 1913. He was raised in a culture which seethed with resentment against the dominant Czechs, and he soon became a Slovakian nationalist.

He studied law in Bratislava, Slovakia's principal city, and organized a group of Catholic university students into what he called the Academic Guard. "It was a paramilitary organization of university students, led by me as supreme commander," he explained in a book he later wrote on the history of Slovakia.

But the Academic Guard was also anti-semitic, according to Frank Nash, a Jew who lived in Bratislava at that time. In a sworn statement he made in 1988, after allegations had been made that Kirschbaum was a Nazi collaborator, Nash said:

> On literally dozens of occasions, I saw Kirschbaum rise up, sometimes on to a table, and lead a group of guards in a chorus of anti-Jewish slogans, like a conductor leading a choir. One typical chant went: 'In Slovakia it will only be good when from every Vrba tree a Jew will be hanging. . . .'
>
> I also saw Kirschbaum on several occasions leading groups of uniformed Academic Guards down main streets in Bratislava, encouraging them to break Jewish store windows and vandalize Jewish homes, which they did.

By 1938, Kirschbaum was writing regularly for fascist newspapers in Slovakia, and his political star was rising. He was one of the men who secretly negotiated with the Germans. Kirschbaum arrived in Berlin on Remembrance Day in 1938, seeking Nazi help to make his dream of an independent Slovakia come true. He was accompanied by Durcansky and by Franz Karmasin, the leader of a Nazi-style storm trooper unit in Slovakia.

The three men met with Nazi Reichsmarshall Hermann Goering, Hitler's industrial chief and right-hand man. Four months later, Joseph Tiso and Hitler signed a declaration of Slovakian "independence." This made Tiso the leader of Slovakia.

As a reward for his role in the "independence" process, Kirschbaum was given the position of secretary-general of the Hlinka party. He held that position until July 1940, when Durcansky was dropped from Tiso's government, and Kirschbaum was dropped along with him.

During the time that Kirschbaum served as secretary-general of the party, the Tiso regime brought in anti-semitic regulations. Jews were banned from the University of Bratislava, where Kirschbaum's Academic Guard was in almost complete control. Jewish industries were systematically expropriated.

It was the duty of the general secretariat, which Kirschbaum headed, to decide who got control of the Jews' property. *Slovak*, the Hlinka party's newspaper, described the general secretariat's role in this process.

It said:

> Neither district secretaries nor other party officers should involve themselves in matters concerning exemption of Jews from their labor obligations, but should refer all matters of this nature to the General Secretariat, the only competent office in this respect.

Kirschbaum's office was also responsible for organizing several lectures and speeches on "aryanization," the process by which Jews were to be excluded from society. Kirschbaum was quoted on this topic in the March 5, 1940, edition of *Slovak*. The newspaper said that Kirschbaum, while speaking to a group of young farmers, said:

> What the Slovak government does today is nothing else but a punishment for political betrayal. . . . It is taking away the property of political profiteers . . . and is excluding Jews from the economic life, and preventing them from further enslaving the Slovak people. . . . When the Jews are touched by a law, we are only punishing the crimes of the members of this race, but not individuals as members of the Jewish religion.

Another newspaper, *Slovenska Pravda*, quoted Kirschbaum in its June 21, 1940, issue as saying:

> In every field there comes a time for reckoning. The Jews will be excluded from business – from wherever they can harm us.

Kirschbaum later maintained that while he was a member of the Hlinka Party, he did not know what the government was doing to the Jews. He said his position of secretary-general was not part of the "inner government." Because he was on the fringes of government, he claimed, he did not know about the laws being passed against the Jews.

"I knew there was some orders restricting the Jewish population in certain fields," said Kirschbaum, "but since it was not my office, I was not interested to read or get information what was it about at this time."

Kirschbaum said he did not read *Slovak*, the fascist newspaper in which he was quoted as making anti-semitic statements. He explained that "if there was something important, my secretary told me, but I didn't have time to read."

By mid-1940, when Kirschbaum was removed from his position as secretary-general, Slovakia's Jews were systematically being stripped of their possessions and their human dignity. But at least they were still alive.

It wasn't until two years later – long after Kirschbaum had lost his position as secretary-general and had left Slovakia for Switzerland to serve as Slovakian chargé d'affaires – that the massive deportation of Jews began.

In 1946, the communist government of Czechoslovakia asked the Allies to send Kirschbaum home for trial as a war criminal, but the Allies said that because he was in Switzerland, they couldn't touch him. But Kirschbaum didn't stay long in his safe haven.

He went to Rome, where he helped fellow Slovakian exiles get visas so they could immigrate to safe countries. Meanwhile, he was tried *in absentia* by a Czechoslovakian "people's court." He was sentenced to 20 years in prison, but by that time he had left Rome, carrying papers which had been issued by the Vatican.

He was refused entry into the United States on the grounds that he had been a Nazi collaborator, but that didn't prevent him from getting into Canada.

He was accepted as an immigrant, and landed in Halifax in November 1949. He soon became active with the Canadian Slovak League, which was founded by Stephen Roman, a Toronto businessman who had come to Canada before the start of the war and earned a fortune in mining and resources. Roman did all he could to promote Slovakian independence, and Kirschbaum became one of his closest allies.

Their efforts on behalf of Slovakia brought them into contact with some of the most powerful politicians in Canada, including Louis St. Laurent, Lester Pearson and Paul Martin Sr. Kirschbaum's high public profile eventually led to media attention.

In 1962, a Czech immigrant named Joseph Cermak read a newspaper story about Kirschbaum. Cermak, angry that

Kirschbaum was enjoying a life of wealth and status in Canada after playing a role in the Tiso regime, began to write articles about Kirschbaum's past in a Czech-language newspaper. The *Canadian Jewish News* picked up the story and published an article describing Kirschbaum as a Nazi collaborator.

Kirschbaum responded by saying:

> I was never pro-Nazi. I was never anti-Jewish. At no time did my political duties in Slovakia have anything to do with the Jewish question. As a matter of fact, the first laws against the Jews were introduced in Slovakia in 1941, some time after I was forced to resign.

The issue died until 1988, when the *Whig-Standard*, a daily newspaper in Kingston, Ontario, ran a 48-page special report titled "The Kirschbaum File." Paul McKay, a former *Whig-Standard* reporter, came across the Kirschbaum story while researching a book on Stephen Roman.

McKay went to Czechoslovakia, where he found plenty of information about Kirschbaum, including newspaper reports of his wartime activities and photos of him in a military-style uniform. When Kirschbaum learned that the *Whig-Standard* intended to publish this material, his lawyers warned the *Whig-Standard* of the possibility of a libel suit.

But the newspaper was not intimidated. It went ahead and published the special section on December 10, 1988, and Kirschbaum did not sue. The threat of legal action, however, did have a chilling effect on other news organizations, and no other newspaper followed the *Whig-Standard*'s lead and picked up the story.

Burnett M. Thall, senior vice-president of *The Toronto Star*, explained why his paper didn't tell its readers about the past life of the prominent Toronto businessman and well-known Slovakian patriot. In a letter to Sol Littman of the Simon Wiesenthal Centre, Thall said:

> The problem, as I understand it, is a legal one. A letter was served on us by Kirschbaum's lawyer warning us that if any allegations were made in *The Star*, he would sue. While this was obviously designed to scare us off, it certainly highlighted the legal dilemma we were in. I suspect this is also the reason no other newspaper felt it could run the article.

And so once again, Kirschbaum's story died in the Canadian news media, and his comfortable life in Toronto continued. He was almost 80 when he went back to Slovakia in 1992 for the first time in more than half a century. By then, the communists had been turfed out, and Kirschbaum had no reason to fear he would be arrested and forced to start serving the 20-year sentence he received from the "people's court" back in 1948.

Czechoslovakia in 1992 was a democracy which was coming part. It had decided to split into two states once more. On January 1, 1993, Slovakia once again became a separate nation.

Kirschbaum must have been happy about that, because this time his beloved Slovakia was a truly independent state, not the "politically notorious" regime it had been when it was ruled by Joseph Tiso and the Nazis.

CHAPTER 10

The Mare of Majdanek

Hermine Braunsteiner had a way with children. She plied them with candy to lure them to their deaths when she worked as a guard at the Majdanek concentration camp in Poland.

She was also notorious for kicking prisoners with her shiny, studded jackboots. The inmates of Majdanek called her "kobyla" – the Polish word for "mare."

Braunsteiner is the only female Nazi war criminal known to have come to Canada. Fortunately, her stay was a brief one, and by the time her secret was discovered in the 1960s, she had moved to the United States.

She was born in Vienna in 1919, the youngest daughter of a chauffeur. She was raised in a strict Roman Catholic family and left home in her early teens to work for a cattle dealer.

Then she applied to the Blue Sisters, a German nursing organization, and if things had turned out differently, she might have gone on to become an angel of mercy. But before her nursing application was processed, she landed a job in a Berlin munitions factory.

That, in turn, led to her joining the SS, and in 1939 she became a guard at the Ravensbruck concentration camp for women. She was transferred to Majdanek in 1942, returned to Ravensbruck two years later, and was still there when Allied troops arrived in 1945. She was held briefly by the British, then returned to Vienna. But food was scarce there so she moved to southern Austria to live with relatives.

War crimes investigators caught up with her in 1948. She was convicted of slapping, kicking and whipping female prisoners at Ravensbruck. No mention was made of her time at Majdanek. She was sentenced to three years in prison, but released after just nine months.

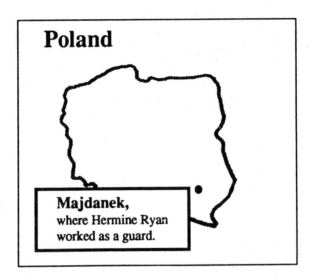

Poland

Majdanek,
where Hermine Ryan
worked as a guard.

She worked in shops and resorts until 1957, when she met Russell Ryan, a 37-year-old American electronics inspector who was vacationing in Austria. She apparently didn't tell him all about her previous life. Hermine and Russell fell in love. They moved to Canada and were married in Halifax in 1958.

Hermine obtained a visa from Canadian authorities with ease, simply by lying about her past. Little is known about their time in Halifax, and the newlyweds moved to the United States early the following year. They settled near New York City. Hermine Ryan became a U.S. citizen in January 1963. Her transformation was complete.

The former Mare of Majdanek had exchanged her starched SS uniforms, crackling whips and shiny jackboots for the lace aprons and muffin tins of an American housewife.

A chance occurrence halfway around the world in 1964 led to her downfall. Austrian Nazi hunter Simon Wiesenthal was in Israel when he was approached by three women in a cafe. They had been inmates in Majdanek and knew that Wiesenthal was tracking down war criminals.

"You must know what happened to Kobyla?" one of the women asked him. Wiesenthal didn't know what she was talking about. He had never heard of the Mare of Majdanek.

"She was the worst of them all," the first woman explained.

One of the other women, tears welling in her eyes, recalled the day that the Mare discovered a small, sobbing child hidden in a prisoner's rucksack. The Mare whipped the child, then shot it through the face. "If they place shards on my eyes when I die," said the weeping woman, "my dead eyes will still see that child's face."

Wiesenthal started looking into the case when he returned to his headquarters in Vienna. He learned that after the war, Hermine Braunsteiner had moved to Carinthia in southern Austria. Wiesenthal sent an agent there.

The agent befriended Hermine's relatives and learned she had married an American named Ryan and was living in Halifax. Wiesenthal contacted a friend in Canada who had survived Auschwitz, asking him to determine Ryan's address in Halifax. The friend wrote back:

> Braunsteiner-Ryan no longer lives in Halifax. She has moved to the United States and lives at 5211 72nd Street, Maspet, Queens, N.Y. That is the address to which her mail is forwarded from Halifax.

Wiesenthal contacted Clyde Farnsworth, Vienna correspondent for *The New York Times*, and told him Ryan's sordid story. Farnsworth replied that if his newspaper published an article about Ryan, "the pressure of public opinion will put the proper authorities into action."

Two weeks later, *Times* reporter Joseph Lelyveld appeared on Ryan's doorstep. She was painting her living room. Lelyveld described her as "a large-boned woman with a stern mouth and blond hair turning gray."

Attired in a sleeveless blouse and pink-and-white striped shorts, Ryan erupted in tears when the reporter confronted her about her past. "This is the end," she replied in heavily-accented English. "This is the end of everything for me."

Ryan admitted she was Hermine Braunsteiner of Majdanek, but said she wanted to put her past behind her. "On the radio all they talk is peace and freedom," she said. "Then 15 or 16 years after, why do they bother people?"

Ryan told Lelyveld she had just been a guard at Majdanek, with no authority. "All I did is what guards do in camps now," she claimed. She told Lelyveld she'd been punished enough for her crimes. "I was in prison three years," she lied. "Three years! Can you imagine? And now they want something again from me?"

Ryan claimed she'd been ill for much of the time she was at Majdanek, and that she'd spent eight months in the camp's infirmary.

Russell Ryan defended her. "My wife, sir, wouldn't hurt a fly," he told the reporter.

> There's no more decent person on this earth. This was a duty she had to perform. It was a conscriptive service. She was not in charge of anything. Absolutely not, as God is my judge.

Ryan complained about his wife's accusers. "These people are just swinging axes at random," he charged. "Didn't they ever hear the expression, 'Let the dead rest?'"

Despite Hermine's fears that "this is the end," she enjoyed four more years of relative peace and obscurity in New York City. But in 1968 the U.S. Justice Department finally moved to revoke her citizenship.

The prosecution accused her of being "a cruel, brutal and sadistic woman who unnecessarily beat and tortured defenseless prisoners." The denaturalization case was based on Ryan's concealment of the fact that she had been in the SS, as well as her failure to report her 1949 conviction for torturing and mistreating inmates at Ravensbruck. "Had the defendant disclosed the true facts of her conviction," the Justice Department said, "she would have been barred from lawful admission into the United States for permanent residence and from naturalization."

TV crews and newspaper reporters besieged Ryan's house. Residents of the predominantly German and Irish neighborhood were hostile to the journalists. Neighbors said they knew nothing of Ryan's background, apart from the 1964 *New York Times* exposé.

Ryan enjoyed a three-year reprieve as the wheels of American justice ground slowly along, but in 1971 she voluntarily gave up her U.S. citizenship. Ryan's decision to do so has never been explained. It may have been a strategic move to prevent a federal court from ruling against her. Such a ruling could have been used against her later, at her deportation hearing.

That hearing began in 1972, and that's when the Mare got to tell her story under oath. She testified that she'd been a guard at several Nazi camps during the war, including Majdanek. She admitted striking prisoners occasionally, but said she only did so "with an open hand."

Ryan said she knew Majdanek was an extermination camp, but claimed she was helpless to prevent the atrocities. "It was not in my power to do anything," she said. "I was too little." She claimed she never saw children at Majdanek.

Several witnesses contradicted Ryan's testimony, including Mary Finkelstein, who identified her from an old photograph. "If her name is Hermine, it's her," cried Finkelstein, pointing at Ryan in the courtroom.

Finkelstein said Ryan was an imposing presence at Majdanek. "She came in with a German uniform, with a stick, with a dog, and once in awhile with a whip."

Finkelstein testified that Ryan once "clobbered" a female prisoner with a stick because the inmate was hunched over. The Mare screamed, "You pig! You goddamn Jew! Stand up straight!" as she beat the woman, Finkelstein recalled. The woman crumpled to the ground "and didn't get up ever."

Eva Konikowski accused Ryan of beating her with a rubber stick and said she still bore the scars. She testified that she saw Ryan and other guards herd children bound for execution into trucks at Majdanek.

The children were "screaming and crying 'Mama.' They gave the children some pieces of candy and the children were taken away to the gas chambers," said Konikowski, who screamed so hard when she saw the children lured to their deaths that she needed surgery on her throat after the war.

A frail, soft-spoken man named Aaron Kaufman, who had been in eight concentration camps, came forward after reading about Ryan in the newspaper. He told the court he saw the Mare whip five women and a child to death at Majdanek, in three separate incidents.

Kaufman said the first two murders occurred in May 1942. He was hauling coal and passed a group of women pulling weeds in a fenced corridor, he recalled.

"Suddenly, Braunsteiner appeared, spoke to the women for a minute, then started beating two of them," Kaufman testified. "Both died." The witness said he was only six yards away when the women were murdered. He knew both victims by name.

When camp officials learned he had witnessed the first two killings, Kaufman said, he was dragged from his quarters and repeatedly lashed across the back.

Kaufman said Ryan murdered two more women in what he called the "second field" at Majdanek. Kaufman was hauling lumber that day, and noticed a group of female inmates who had interrupted their work to talk. Incensed by the women's behavior, Ryan whipped two of them to death, Kaufman said.

He observed the third incident while he pulled a wagonload of food to what was called "field five." Kaufman was blocked at the gate by hundreds of frantic women inmates.

"Braunsteiner was telling the ladies they had to give their children away because the children were going to a summer camp where they would get milk two times a day," recalled Kaufman. "The mothers didn't want to give up their children because they knew what would happen."

Ryan then beat a woman and her child to death, Kaufman said.

One of the final witnesses at Ryan's deportation hearing was Danuta Czaykowska-Medryk, a Warsaw dentist who came to New York to testify. She said she saw Ryan select Jewish women for execution in August 1943. That same month, Ryan threw Jewish children onto a truck bound for the gas chambers, the witness said.

"One policewoman refused to help, and Braunsteiner hit her across the face," Czaykowska-Medryk recalled. The witness said Ryan frequently beat, kicked and whipped prisoners at Majdanek, and well deserved her nickname as the Mare. "The moment I walked in, I recognized her," Czaykowska-Medryk testified.

"Easy to say," scoffed Ryan, loud enough for spectators to hear.

The U.S. government's bid to deport Ryan was successful. She was extradited to West Germany in 1973. In 1975, she and 16 co-defendants went on trial in Dusseldorf, charged with the murder of "at least 1,181 prisoners" and complicity in the murder of 705 others.

Ryan remained free on bail for much of the trial, living in a shoebox apartment near the Dusseldorf courthouse. Her faithful husband moved to West Germany in 1977 to be near her.

But in June 1979, as judgment day neared, the court ordered Hermine and three co-defendants to be held in custody. The judge agreed with the prosecution that Ryan could expect a life sentence, and was therefore a flight risk.

On June 30, 1981, Ryan was convicted of murder and sentenced to life in prison. She was the only defendant at the Dusseldorf trial to receive a life sentence. At last report, the Mare was still in a German prison.

Her husband, faithful to the end, blamed her conviction on American Jews. "They demand these trials," Russell Ryan concluded, "and this is what happens."

CHAPTER 11

He Sewed While Others Shot

A Nazi-led police battalion which slaughtered an estimated 130,000 Jews, gypsies and others in Eastern Europe in 1941 included one man who ended up in Canada.

He was Joseph Kisielaitis, who admitted serving in the murderous unit, but denied he had done anything wrong. He presented himself as a nobody who minded his own business and didn't even know what was going on, let alone take part in it.

Kisielaitis said he just worked as a tailor. He claimed that while the killing was going on, he spent his time cutting cloth and sewing uniforms. He said he had no idea the men who wore those uniforms were going out each day to kill innocent people.

He said it wasn't until many years later that he found out what happened, despite the fact that the killing spree carried out by his colleagues wasn't an isolated incident. It was a planned, systematic slaughter. It lasted seven months, and Kisielaitis was right in the middle of it, somehow managing to remain blissfully unaware of what was happening as he dutifully wielded his needle and thread.

Some of the worst of the killing took place in the Lithuanian capital city of Kaunas, where members of the battalion took 100 Jews at a time into the hills, stripped them of their clothes and jewelry, and forced them to dig their own graves. Then the killers shot the Jews with machine guns, murdering as many as 9,200 people in a single day.

The Canadian government apparently accepted Kisielaitis' explanation, since it took no action against him after it became aware of his background. But the American government considered him a war criminal, and the U.S. Justice Department was in the process of kicking him out of the country in the mid-1980s when he slipped across the border and found sanctuary in a small Alberta town.

Kisielaitis, who learned the art of tailoring at the age of 13 when he was apprenticed to a Jewish tailor, said he was in his late teens when he became a member of the police battalion in Nazi-controlled Lithuania. He said he was below the rank of private, and that he did what he was told to do – sit in a room and make uniforms.

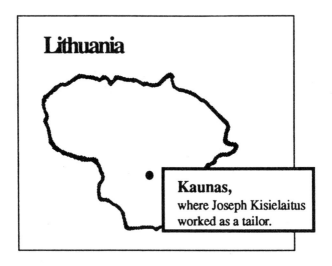

Lithuania

Kaunas,
where Joseph Kisielaitus worked as a tailor.

He did admit, however, that he was once part of a team that carried ammunition to soldiers protecting a peat-cutting crew. But Kisielaitis said his role in such military operations was limited, partly because he was needed as a tailor, and partly because he had an unusual physical disability.

He claimed he was unable to close just one eye. If he tried to close one eye, he said, they both closed. That meant he couldn't sight a rifle – but somehow he was able to thread a needle, a skill required of any tailor.

A Russian ambush ended Kisielaitis' police career. He was machine-gunned in the arms and chest in an attack which left 12 of his comrades dead. He was discharged from the army and continued working as a tailor until 1944 when he, his parents and sisters fled to Germany to escape the advancing Russians.

The family eventually ended up in a displaced persons' camp. That's where Kisielaitis met his wife Julia, and they soon had a daughter born in the camp. Kisielaitis' opportunity to leave the camp came when a tailoring union sent a delegation looking for people to work in Canada. Kisielaitis passed a proficiency exam and immigrated with his family in 1948.

He settled in Montreal, where he continued working as a tailor and learned the fur business. He became a Canadian citizen in 1953.

Ten years later, a better job opportunity as foreman at the Supreme Coat Company took him south of the border to Worcester, Massachusetts. Later, Kisielaitis worked for Cohen Tailoring and eventually became a partner in the business. When his partner retired in the late 1970s, Kisielaitis took over and named it Joseph's Tailoring.

For 21 years, Kisielaitis and his family lived a quiet life in Massachusetts, but in 1981 his life became very public when the United States Justice Department started investigating him. The department claimed that Kisielaitis had omitted some important information from his application for a visa to enter the United States in 1963.

The Soviets tipped off the Justice Department's Office of Special Investigations, which was established by the Justice Department in 1978 to find and prosecute war criminals in the U.S.

A document supplied by the Soviets contained the names of people said to be members of the killing battalion, which was known as the Schutzmannschaft. One of the names on the list was "Juozas Kisielaitis." Asked if the name on the list was his, Kisielaitis admitted that it was. But he said he had never heard the word "Schutzmannschaft" until the Justice Department told him what it was.

He said he knew the military unit he served in as the 12th Lithuanian Battalion. He denied that it had any German officers, but Neal Sher, director of the Office of Special Investigations, said the unit was under the command of Major Franz Lechthaler, head of the Nazi police in the German 11th Reserve Battalion. After the war, Lechthaler was convicted of war crimes.

Kisielaitis denied concealing information on his visa application. "The questions on the form only dealt with whether you were in the German army or in a political party," he said, "and those I answered truthfully. I wasn't asked about any Lithuanian battalion."

Later, however, Kisielaitis' lawyer, Robert Shumway, conceded that certain mis-statements were made, but insisted this was no reason to brand the man a Nazi war criminal. The lawyer said Kisielaitis was just "a little guy."

The question of Kisielaitis' membership in the battalion was never in dispute. While testifying in the 1982 deportation hearing of Jurgis Juodis, an officer of the Schutzmannschaft who was also being prosecuted by the U.S. Justice Department, Kisielaitis admitted being a member of the police unit.

Since mere membership in the battalion made an applicant ineligible to enter the United States, the Justice Department started deportation proceedings against Kisielaitis in June 1984.

News coverage of the story generated more publicity than Kisielaitis could handle. By that point he was in his mid-60s. Before the deportation proceedings against him were concluded, Kisielaitis quietly sold his business and home in Massachusetts and moved back to Canada.

He lived in obscurity for about 10 months, until the U.S. Justice Department issued a press release saying Kisielaitis had fled to Canada. *The New York Times* reported on April 30, 1985, that Kisielaitis "went to Canada recently rather than face charges that he assisted the Nazis in persecuting Jews while he served in the Schutzmannschaft, a military battalion in his native Lithuania." On the same day, a report by United Press International (UPI) said the Canadian government would act against Kisielaitis if the allegation was found to be true.

"If it can be proved Kisielaitis lied about his wartime activities on entering Canada after the war," UPI said, "he could be stripped of his Canadian citizenship and ordered deported back to the United States or Lithuania."

Although the Canadian government admitted in May 1985 knowing that Kisielaitis was back in Canada, then-Immigration Minister Flora MacDonald denied knowing his exact whereabouts. She said the matter would be left up to the newly established Deschênes commission for investigation.

But the U. S. Justice Department had a good idea where Kisielaitis was, and issued another press release saying he was in the Calgary area. Happy to be rid of Kisielaitis, Neal Sher of the OSI said, "He's Canada's problem now."

That didn't satisfy Kisielaitis' lawyer, Robert Shumway, who was infuriated with the Justice Department's tactics of issuing news releases, especially since negotiations to work out a deal were under way.

Shumway told the *Worcester Telegram* that a proposed agreement would have had Kisielaitis admit that he made mis-statements on his visa application. In return, the U.S. would not give any information it had on Kisielaitis to Canadian authorities, and would ensure that he got his U.S. social security payments.

Apparently the Justice Department had one other stipulation, and that was to issue a press release to put the outcome of the case before the public. Kisielaitis didn't want any more publicity, so the deal fell through.

When the U.S. Justice Department went ahead with the news release anyway and said Kisielaitis was in the Calgary area, the Canadian news media took up the case. Reporters soon discovered that Kisielaitis and his wife were living in Brooks, Alberta, a small community about 100 miles southeast of Calgary.

They had been living with Kisielaitis' sister, Anna Albright, since leaving the United States the previous summer. He had been working at his nephew's laundry shop in the nearby community of Duchess, Alberta.

Shumway launched an attack against the U.S. Justice Department. "They are describing this poor bastard as a wanted Nazi war criminal," he complained. "He's wanted nowhere by anyone for anything. He has never been accused anywhere by anyone of anything. He has never done anything, anywhere to anyone."

Kisielaitis continued to maintained his innocence, saying: "How was I, a soldier below the rank of private, to know of high-level command structures? I was a tailor."

How indeed?

The *Calgary Herald* obtained photocopies of documents listing Kisielaitis as "a soldier who took part in missions responsible for the massacre of thousands of Jews and Gypsies."

Charles Allen, an authority on war criminals in the United States, said the documents provided "conclusive proof" that

Kisielaitis had left on a mission with the battalion, "unless he fell down and got sick that day as he was walking out of the camp."

One list was said to have ended with the names of two privates and a corporal who did not take part in the mission. Kisielaitis' name was not one of them, suggesting that he did go on the mission. Shumway countered by saying that the lists didn't necessarily prove anything. He said the documents covered a limited time frame, and whoever was providing them was being very selective.

Kisielaitis had his own theory about who was causing all his trouble. He blamed the Soviets. "The plan of the KGB is to destroy those that fled," he said. "They are shouting 'Nazi' when not even all Germans were Nazis."

While the U.S. Justice Department was saying that Kisielaitis fled the United States to avoid deportation, Kisielaitis himself maintained he simply couldn't take any more publicity, and left to escape media attention.

U.S. officials insisted that steps would be taken so Kisielaitis could never enter the United States again, but he continued to cross the border, visiting friends, relatives and his lawyer in Worcester.

Kisielaitis' present whereabouts are unknown. The *Calgary Herald* lost interest in the story in 1985, when it is believed Kisielaitis returned to Montreal, where his wife had family. The news media didn't make a big fuss over the fact that the suspected war criminal was in Montreal, so Kisielaitis finally got what he wanted – an end to publicity about his past, and the chance to live out his remaining days quietly.

CHAPTER 12

At the End of His Rope

Daisy Laak couldn't find her husband when she came home one afternoon in the summer of 1960. She went to the garage to see if the car was gone, and found him hanging from the rafters.

She tugged frantically on the loose end of the clothesline around his neck, and her husband's body fell on top of her. She tried to revive him, but it was no use. An ambulance came, and then a coroner.

Alexander Laak was pronounced dead at 6:55 p.m. on September 6, 1960. The 53-year-old immigrant from Estonia had committed suicide, just a week after the Soviet Union accused him of being a war criminal.

The Soviets, who took control of Estonia and the other Baltic states when they drove the Germans out in 1944, considered people who had collaborated with the Nazis to be war criminals. They had been looking for Laak for years, and found he was living in suburban Winnipeg after intercepting a letter Laak had written to his mother back home in Estonia.

Since the Canadian authorities were unlikely to agree to a quiet extradition, the Soviets decided to publicize the case, to put pressure on Ottawa, and on Laak himself, to make it hard for him to live in peace in his new country.

The Soviet news agency *Tass* sent out a story accusing Canada of providing sanctuary for Laak. *Tass* said that as the commandant of a Nazi concentration camp in Estonia, Laak had been responsible for the deaths of more than 3,000 people in 1942 and 1943. The victims were said to be scientists, physicians, merchants, industrial executives and bank directors from Czechoslovakia and Germany. Many of them were said to be Jews and women.

The Soviets said that in 1944, the Nazis dug up the corpses and burned them, to cover up the mass executions. *Tass* reported that human bones and ashes were found scattered around the area. The news agency also claimed Laak had stolen valuables from the concentration camp victims, sold them and used the money to pay for his house in Canada.

The Winnipeg *Free Press* picked up the story. In its initial report, the newspaper repeated the Soviet claims but didn't name Laak. The story referred to him only as a "city man." Reporters soon tracked him down, however, and Laak agreed to be interviewed for a second story, on condition that his name not be published.

In that story, Laak maintained that the Nazis had kept their activities at the concentration camp secret, and that he had never even heard of the camp until after the war.

The camp was known as Jagala. It was one of 37 concentration camps which the Nazis operated in Estonia, and in which some 125,000 people were killed.

Laak didn't deny working for the Nazis, but claimed he had held an honorable job. He said he was the warden of the central prison in Tallinn, the Estonian capital. Laak said he was only in charge of convicts, not political prisoners.

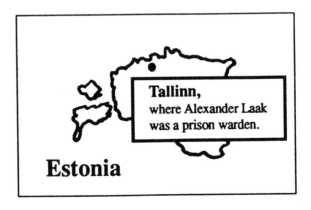

Tallinn, where Alexander Laak was a prison warden.

Estonia

Laak tried to make it sound as if the Tallinn prison was a million miles from Jagala. He said he had been living a "peaceful life" with his family "far from where the executions were reported to have taken place" at Jagala.

In fact, Jagala was only about 15 miles from to Tallinn. It was hard to believe that the warden of the Tallinn prison would have been unaware of Jagala. It was also hard to believe that the Nazis would have gone to the trouble of keeping "convicts" separate from Jews and others who were persecuted for racial and political reasons.

Laak insisted he was an innocent man, but Arthur Drache, one of the reporters who interviewed Laak, didn't believe him. "Laak said he was the warden of a penitentiary, much like the Canadian Stony Mountain Penitentiary," Drache recalled recently. "But he said it had Jews and gypsies, and that a lot of them died there. That's what stands out in my mind."

Laak fled the advancing Russians in 1944. He went to Germany, and after the war worked briefly for the Royal Air Force. In 1948 he made his way to Canada via Genoa, Italy.

He soon got a job as a laborer for Ontario Hydro, earning 65 cents an hour. Daisy Laak said her husband scrimped and saved to bring her, their three sons and one daughter to Canada from Germany about eight months after his arrival.

In 1950 the Laaks moved to Winnipeg, where Daisy worked as a domestic helper and the sons delivered newspapers. Laak started work as a janitor at the Royal Canadian Air Force base. In 1959 the Laaks bought their house at 272 Guildford Street in the Winnipeg suburb of St. James. A year later, the Soviets found out where he was.

Daisy Laak was especially outraged by the Soviet claims that the house had been paid for with money stolen from Jagala execution victims. "It took us 12 years to get it," she bitterly responded. "I haven't even got a fur coat. Yet they said we took money away."

The fuss might have blown over if a Winnipeg radio station hadn't picked up the story. *CKY* rehashed the information which had been put out by *Tass* and the *Free Press*, but the radio station went one step further.

It revealed Laak's identity.

Suddenly everyone knew who the alleged war criminal was. Three days later, Laak hanged himself.

His suicide turned what had been a local story into a national and international one. *The Globe and Mail* picked it up, and then *The New York Times* ran a piece saying that the former commandant of the Jagala concentration camp was dead.

Gisela Herzl, a New York resident, recognized Laak from his picture in the paper. Herzl phoned the Canadian consulate and offered to provide additional information about Laak, but she didn't get a warm reception.

"The consulate denied Laak was a collaborator," Herzl recalled recently. "They said he was an outstanding Canadian citizen living in Winnipeg." Frustrated at the Canadian consulate's response, Herzl told her story to the Winnipeg *Free Press*, which published it four days after Laak's death.

Herzl, a Czechoslovakian Jew who was 22 years old when she was arrested in 1942, said she was in the Jagala concentration camp for more than a year. She recalled the first time she saw Laak.

"He had large, large eyes, and a round head," Herzl remembered. "He had a fairly good figure. He was like a strong soldier." Herzl said Laak was the "head man" of the camp. She never saw him beat or shoot anyone, but was "100 per cent sure he knew what was going on."

Herzl said she and others once asked Laak where their families were. "He told us that we should not worry about them, that they have it much better than we. They don't have to work anymore." Herzl took that to mean that the family members were dead.

Elizabeth Steinlauf also remembered Laak. Steinlauf, a German Jew, was arrested in Berlin and sent to Jagala, where she saw Laak in his role as commandant. She also saw him in the same role at the central prison in Tallinn when she was transferred there.

Steinlauf, like Herzl, ended up in New York City, and also saw Laak's photo in *The New York Times* in 1960. Unlike Herzl, Steinlauf didn't speak publicly about it at the time. She did, however, agree to discuss her wartime experiences when she was contacted recently by telephone.

"There were about 1,200 people," Steinlauf recalled of her days at Jagala.

> They came with big wagons and they put people on. We happened to be the last ones, because we were ordered to clean out the railway station. I assumed that because we were the last ones that everybody was there already. I found out after

the war they were killed. They were shot. There were only 125 people left.

Steinlauf said that shortly after she arrived at the Jagala camp, her valuables were confiscated:

> They lined us up. I was a pretty young girl, 15 or 16, and had golden earrings with the heart, you know those children things. I still had them in my ear. They ripped them out.

Steinlauf said conditions in Jagala were deplorable. "There were open bunks, three levels of not bunk beds, just slabs of wood. The windows were mostly open and it was very cold."

Steinlauf spent much of her time hiding from Laak and his staff.

"I tried to stay away as much as I could," she said.

> Laak was miserable, miserable. If he didn't like someone he hit them. I saw him going with the whip. If he didn't like someone he would whip them for no apparent reason. He also had underlings who did a lot of his dirty work for him.

Steinlauf said Laak oversaw the selection of prisoners to be executed:

> Laak took away maybe 60 or 70 women. My girlfriend's mother was one of them, and my girlfriend begged Laak to let her go with her mother, and he didn't let her go. They were all shot.

An Ontario woman came forward to say Laak was the commandant, after recognizing him from a picture in a newspaper. Greta Zarkower, a Jew from Prague who was arrested in 1942, told The Canadian Press that "Laak was wearing the SS uniform, and was in charge. Laak and his men took all our valuables, even our rings and watches."

Seven months after Laak's death, Ralf Gerrets, the assistant commandant of the Jagala camp, was put on trial by the Soviets in Estonia, along with Jan Vijk, a Jagala camp guard. A third defendant, Ain Erwin Mere, was tried *in absentia*. He was said to have been the former head of the Estonian security police, but he was living in London and the British refused to extradite him. All three defendants were convicted after a six-day trial. Gerrets and Vijk were executed by a firing squad.

During the trial, Gerrets provided details of how Jagala operated. He said trains arrived regularly from Czechoslovakia with prisoners, most of whom were eventually executed. During a typical operation, a busload of 40 prisoners would be driven from the camp to a 10-foot trench dug nearby. A guard would order the prisoners to undress. Six to 10 people were forced to lie down side by side in the trench and shot.

Then the next group was ordered to lie down on the dead bodies, and they were shot. Gerrets said he usually took the victims' valuables for the security police benefit fund.

During the trial, six Czech survivors of the Jagala camp told the court their train was met by Laak, Gerrets and others. Gerrets claimed Laak was the principal man to blame for the killings, but it appears the commandant might have had a small bit of human compassion.

Jan Vijk testified that Laak ordered him to shoot several gypsy children, ranging in age from 3 to 5. "Laak couldn't do it," Vijk said, "because of the big, wide eyes" of the children.

The story didn't end after Laak's death in 1960. Eleven years later, a Jerusalem-based author named Michael Elkins wrote a book titled *Forged in Fury*. Elkins claimed that an Israeli agent forced Alexander Laak to hang himself.

"Arnie Berg flew from South America to Canada, and on to Winnipeg, to arrive before Alexander Laak could run further for fear of retribution for the hundred thousand Jews he ordered killed when he had been commandant of the Jagala death camp," Elkins wrote.

> Berg took his man into the garage of Laak's suburban home, and told Laak just how he intended to kill him – and his wife when she got home from the cinema. After fifteen minutes of this, Laak begged for the mercy of being allowed to kill himself 'decently.'
>
> So Berg gave him a rope; and left him hanging there . . . a clear case of suicide.

Elkins' book went largely unnoticed in Canada for almost two decades, but in 1990 the Winnipeg *Free Press* published an article about Elkins' theory. The article caught the eye of Fred Woodward, a Winnipeg man who thought Elkins' story just might be true.

"I don't believe it was suicide, because he didn't leave a note," said Woodward. "I feel it is an injustice when an Israeli agent killed Laak when he hadn't even been tried and found guilty of the crime they killed him for."

Woodward's suspicions led to an RCMP inquiry into the old case, but the Mounties said they could find no evidence to support Elkins' allegations. They concluded that Laak's death had been what it seemed to be – a suicide.

A coroner's jury reached the same conclusion at an inquest back in 1960, just eight days after Laak died. The jury ruled out the possibility of foul play after a pathologist testified there were no marks on the body to indicate anyone else had been involved.

Radio Moscow apparently also believed Laak had taken his own life. In a report broadcast shortly after his death, the Soviet radio station offered this gloating epitaph:

> Laak cravenly hung himself in his garage, obviously afraid to face the responsibility of his crimes. Like the scorpion, this hardened murderer took his own life. His nerves seemed to get the better of him.

CHAPTER 13

The Freedom Fighter

When the Soviets accused Dmytro Kupyak of murdering women, children and old people in his native Ukraine while the Nazis were in power, he didn't run for cover. He welcomed the chance to talk to reporters, and used the media to defend himself.

At one point, after the Soviets had been harassing him for several years, the cocky Kupyak even called a news conference to publicly invite Soviet Premier Alexei Kosygin to come to Canada and debate. Kupyak said he'd like to square off against Kosygin on the question of who the real criminals were – people like himself, who had fought for Ukrainian freedom and independence, or the communists, who trampled on human rights and forced Ukraine to become part of the U.S.S.R.?

His spirited response to the Soviet allegations helped Kupyak win the nomination of the Progressive-Conservative party for the riding of Toronto-Lakeshore in the 1972 federal election. He lost, but he got almost 10,000 votes, which was 50 percent more than the Tory candidate got in the previous election.

Kupyak admitted later that he didn't expected to win, but that running for Parliament was his way of showing the Soviets that a free man in a free country had nothing to fear from the communists and their lies.

He also wrote an autobiography in which he set out in detail what he had done during the war. The book, not suprisingly, portrayed him in a favorable light. And in the summer of 1994, at the age of 75, he was interviewed by a television crew from his homeland, where he had become a minor celebrity after he arranged to have his book distributed in Ukraine.

Kupyak said the Soviets started spreading lies about him in the early 1960s to undermine the growing strength of Ukrainian nationalism in Canada. He had been part of that movement, and had built a 450-seat restaurant in Toronto which featured the food, music and atmosphere of his native land.

Kupyak said if he had been a factory worker, the Soviets wouldn't have bothered him. He felt they were picking on him because he was well known, and they wanted to show that Ukrainian nationalists "were not so innocent. They wanted Canadians to think that we were bandits and robbers and murderers."

He had seen others accused of being war criminals by the Soviets make themselves look guilty by refusing to comment to the press. He recalled that,

> one man choked himself in a car, and one man hanged himself [that was Alexander Laak]. I don't know if they did it themselves, or the Russians helped them, but the idea was to put them under pressure – psychological pressure – and they tried the same technique with me.

> They hoped I'd finish myself off, and that would be proof of my guilt. But I decided to fight back. I had survived the war because I was hard. I was determined. I was strong.

Kupyak began to speak out publicly in 1964, when a story was carried by Reuters news service and picked up by the Canadian news media. The story said the Soviets were demanding that the Canadian government send Kupyak back to Ukraine so he could be put on trial for war crimes. It claimed that he was hiding "somewhere in Canada."

Kupyak laughed at that. He wasn't hiding. He was a prominent member of the Ukrainian-Canadian community, and when he got a call from a reporter at the Toronto *Telegram*, he invited the caller to his restaurant, the Mayfair Inn on The Queensway in Etobicoke. Soon other newspaper reporters showed up, along with photographers and TV crews, and Kupyak spent hours responding to their questions.

In fact, he got a kick out of it, and started a scrap book which grew thicker over the years as he kept up a running battle with the communists through the news media. He clipped out articles which called him "a man with guts" and "the Ukrainian the Soviets hate most in Canada."

He acknowledged that he had killed people during the war, but said he had done so in battle, while fighting the Nazis and communists. He said the Germans and the Russians were both oppressors who had taken over Ukraine, and he considered them both the enemy.

He was proud of the fact that he was born on November 6, 1918, just six days after the establishment of the short-lived West Ukrainian People's Republic. "The fact that I was born a free man in an independent Ukrainian state determined my character and my attitude," he said.

He recalled how the Poles moved into Ukraine soon after it declared its independence after the First World War, and how Ukrainians were prosecuted by Polish courts for such "crimes" as teaching the Ukrainian language to the children and trying to preserve the country's customs.

The Polish oppressors were followed by the Russians at the start of the Second World War, and then by the Nazis, and then the Russians again, in a bewildering string of flip-flops which left patriotic groups like the Organization of National Unity – which he eventually joined – constantly fighting one enemy or another.

"They killed us and we killed them," he explained matter-of-factly as he described the activities of a band of about 20 men he led in the 1940s, first against the Nazis, and then against the Russians.

He told how he and his poorly-equipped guerillas killed the enemy to get their bullets and medicine. He told how his parents were shipped off to Siberia by the Russians, and how the Gestapo ordered his brother's body to be dug up and left to rot on the ground, as warning to others who dared to fight against the Nazis.

"It was terrible, just terrible," he said of those days. "We were fighting like hell. We were fighting for our existence." He admitted that innocent people were killed in the desperate struggle, but said they were never intentionally targeted by the patriots.

He asked reporters what they would do if they saw thousands of Russian paratroops floating down from the sky over Toronto. When the reporters said they would join the Canadian army and fight for their homeland, he asked them if they would fight the Russians by shooting Canadian women, children and elderly people. When they replied that they would never do that, Kupyak told them: "You have answered your own question. You wouldn't do that, and we didn't do that either."

But that's not the way the Soviets told it. According to their version of the truth, Kupyak belonged to a "so-called nationalist anti-Ukrainian and anti-Soviet organization which, pretending to care for Ukrainians, was the tool for fascists to impose their rule over the Ukraine."

The Russians claimed that "Kupyak committed murders and acted as hangman and butcher for the German fascist armies during their intervention on Soviet territory."

The Soviets accused Kupyak of leading a gang of cut-throats who did terrible things, such as shooting a teacher and throwing her body down a well, and burning a village which contained 300 homes. The Soviets went into considerable detail. One of the Soviet allegations went like this:

> In the middle of August 1944, Kupyak learned that 12 women with children, whose ages ranged from 6 to 15, were hiding in a deserted farm at the Vodai hamlet near the village of Grabov, Bug District. Kupyak ordered that the hut be surrounded, set fire to and machine-gunned. Several persons tried to run out of the burning structure but were killed on the spot.
>
> Fifteen-year-old Stefa Babitchuk, whose clothes had caught fire, managed to run several meters from the conflagration. She was caught, her eyes gouged out, and, by Kupyak's order, she was thrust into the fire. A boy by the name of Zhepya Sen, who tried to escape the flames, was hit with an axe that hacked off his left arm, and still alive, he was flung into the flames.

Kupyak was 21 when the Russians arrived in 1939 in the part of western Ukraine in which he lived. He was already active in the community and interested in Ukrainian nationalism, so the Russians tried to persuade him to head up a communist youth organization and win the support of the local people.

When he refused, the communists tried to arrest him, but he escaped and joined an underground movement devoted to winning Ukrainian independence. In retaliation, he said, his parents were sent to Siberia.

When the Germans attacked the Soviets in 1941 and took control of the Lvov area in western Ukraine, Kupyak said, the underground leaders proclaimed independence, but the Nazis soon cracked down.

So the patriots started fighting against the Nazis. Kupyak said that during this period he was inactive in the resistance and went to business college, but in 1943 he helped two Ukrainian leaders escape from jail, "and then I was on the run from the Gestapo."

He said he kept fighting against the Nazis until they were driven out in 1944 by the returning Russians. Then he and the others fought against the Russians once again, hoping that the Allies would attack the communists as soon as the Nazis were defeated, and that this would lead to Ukrainian independence.

The Soviets version of those events went this way:

> During the war, Kupyak graduated from a school of professional hangmen conducted by his Nazi bosses. In the period of two years, from 1941 to 1943, he was chief of police of the Lvov district. After the fascists were driven out of the Ukraine, Kupyak headed a gang called Kalyeh. It was this gang that terrorized the local neighborhood until 1945.

The Soviets tried Kupyak *in absentia* in 1968, and during the 40-day trial they brought forward many witnesses to testify against him and others accused of war crimes. More evidence was collected in 1982, and much of it centred on the Soviet claim that Kupyak was particularly cruel to Polish people who lived in the area.

Typical was a statement released by the Soviets quoting a man named Peter Smaga, who claimed he was part of Kupyak's "gang" during the war. Smaga said:

> In the spring of '44, when our region was still under the German occupation, Dimitri got me involved and was created by him a group of bandits, which was involved in murder and theft of the Soviet citizens. . . .
>
> Dimitri was armed with a machine gun and a pistol. I was involved in many crimes with his group. For that I was sentenced, which I have completed. . . .
>
> The whole thing happened like this. In August of 1944, when Dimitri ordered his group, Michail and Bogdan and a third guy whose name I don't remember and myself to go to the village and kill families of the Polish nationality, Fedorukov and Yasinskiy.
>
> I'd like to mention that Dimitri constantly reminded his group that Pollacks are enemies of Ukrainians and that they have to be killed. Before we went on a mission, Dimitri himself asked me to show him the houses where they lived. Also, he ordered me to carefully check other houses and attics of those families because members of other Polish families might be hiding there, and they would have to be killed also. . . .
>
> Michail knocked at the Fedorukov house. . . . In a few minutes I heard 5 or 6 gunshots. . . . Bogdan said that the girls should

not have been killed. Michail answered that Dimitri ordered them to kill all, and that is what they would do.

In 1945, Kupyak said, after it became clear the Western Allies were not going to attack the Soviets and that they were too strong for the Ukrainians to defeat on their own, the patriots consoled themselves with the thought that "other generations would follow, and some day we would win."

He headed west, passing himself off as a Pole, and eventually made his way into Czechoslovakia and then into Germany, where he spent a year in school. Then he went on to Great Britain, where he got another year's education, concentrating on business subjects and learning English.

In 1948, he came to Canada. He arrived in Halifax, and was soon working in a general store in Vilna, Alberta. Soon he moved to Edmonton, bought his own store and married a Canadian-Ukrainian woman. He sold the store in 1956, moved to Toronto and bought a small restaurant. He sold it and bought another restaurant in 1960, tore it down and built the Mayfair, which did well and eventually enabled Kupyak to move to a farm northwest of Toronto to enjoy a comfortable retirement.

It was at the Mayfair that he met the press for the first time back in 1964, after the Soviet allegations went out over the news wire. It was a Friday afternoon, and the next day the media were full of stories.

The article on page one of the *Telegram* said, "Russians Say City Man War Criminal." A photo in *The Globe and Mail* showed an angry Kupyak denying the Soviet charges. The headline in *The St. Catharines Standard* was, "Toronto Man Says War Crimes Charges Are a Communist Smear."

He wondered what was going to happen at his restaurant on Monday, and for a while he even thought about keeping the doors shut because people might not want to come to a place run by "this war criminal." But he decided to prepare the food, got dressed in his best suit, and waited to see what would happen.

"We didn't open until lunch. By 11:30," he recalled,

the parking lot was already half-full. By noon there was no room in the parking lot. The place was packed. I walked around and people were smiling and they started to clap. They called me over and patted me on the back and they called out, 'Good for you, Dmytro! Give them Ruskies hell!' I knew I had won.

The Action
Begins

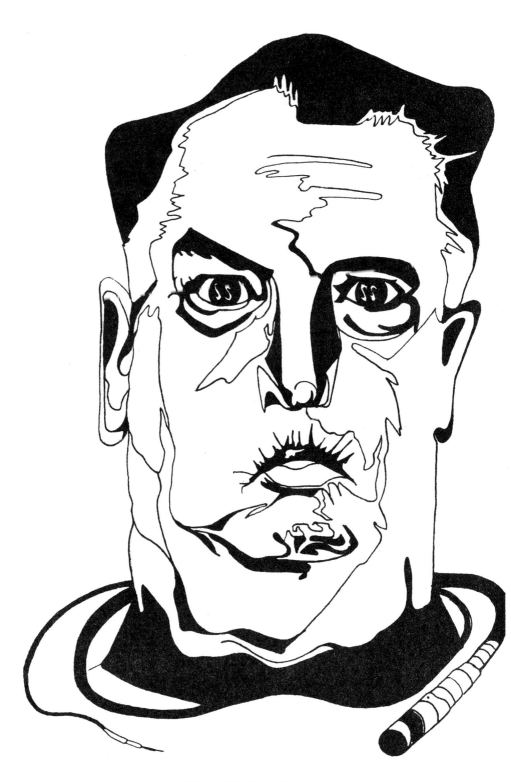

Albert Helmut Rauca

CHAPTER 14

An Old Black Crow

Albert Helmut Rauca was an SS master sergeant with a huge Alsatian dog and a metal-tipped whip. He sent thousands of Lithuanian Jews to their deaths with a casual nod of his head or a slight gesture with his hand, but if you'd seen him in 1950, when he arrived in Canada, you would never have known it.

Rauca seemed to be a harmless and humble fellow when he climbed off a passenger ship in Halifax on December 30, 1950, to start a new life in a new country. He spent his first year working on a tobacco farm in southern Ontario. Then he moved to Toronto, where he took a string of menial jobs and ran a couple of small businesses. Eventually he saved enough money to buy a half-interest in a motel in Huntville, Ontario. He ran that business for 16 years. Then he retired.

Ten years later, when he was 73 years old, Rauca was living a quiet life in north Toronto when he was picked up by the RCMP. When the Mounties arrived just before noon on June 17, 1982, they found Rauca painting the sash on a basement window. They briefly questioned the hefty but fit-looking suspect, to make sure they had the right man. Then they took him to the RCMP regional headquarters in downtown Toronto.

From there, the Mounties drove him to the Ontario Supreme Court, where he stood in the prisoner's box wearing a blue blazer, grey slacks, a shirt and a tie. He wore his white hair brushed straight back. He was arraigned by Associate Chief Justice William Parker on a charge which shocked onlookers. There had never before been such a case in a Canadian courtroom, and the size of the alleged crime was stunning.

Rauca was accused of aiding and abetting the murder of 10,500 persons on or about October 28, 1941, in Kaunas, Lithuania.

In the heavy German accent which he retained despite the fact that he had been in Canada for more than three decades, Rauca said he understood the proceedings. Then he was remanded until the following Monday for a bail hearing, and the Mounties took him away in handcuffs to the Don Jail.

The arrest of Albert Rauca came 21 years after the West Germans first asked the Canadian government to extradite him. The West German prosecutor's office wanted to put him on trial for war crimes, and extradition from Canada was the first step, but it was a long time in coming.

The trial promised to be a sensational affair, perhaps the most spectacular war crimes case since Adolph Eichmann was tried and hanged by the Israelis in the early 1960s. Witnesses from Israel, Lithuania, South Africa and other parts of the world were scheduled to testify against Rauca, who was said to have been a member of an "einsatzgruppe," a Nazi killing squad sent into Lithuania behind the advancing German army. The nominal duty of the einsatzgruppe was to maintain law and order, but in fact its task was to kill Jews.

Rauca was born and raised in the Saxony region of Germany. At the age of 20 he became a district police officer, and four years later he joined the Nazi party. In 1936 he was transferred to the SS, the quasi-military organization whose members were nicknamed the "black crows" because they wore black uniforms and high black boots. The SS was noted for its brutality and fanaticism, and it was the SS which provided the leaders of the einsatzgruppe killing squads.

Witnesses remembered that in Kaunas, a major Lithuanian city which had a large Jewish population, Rauca ordered long lines of Jews to walk past him, as he stood with his dog and his whip and casually appraised each Jew. He split them into two groups. He sent the children and the adults who were old and weak to be shot immediately. The rest, who looked like they were strong enough to work, were sent to a labor camp.

Rauca was also said to have commanded a mass-killing action known as Operation Intellectual, which involved the extermination of many of the better-educated Jews of Kaunas. About 500 people were forced to strip and stand at the edge of an open grave, where they were mowed down by machine-gun fire. Witnesses recalled that Rauca personally gave the orders in this mass murder.

On another occasion, he was also seen shooting a Jew because a silver fork had been found buried in his backyard. This was after the Nazis had ordered the Jews to turn in all their valuables.

Five people in Israel identified him from a photo line-up of more than 100 pictures. Documents bearing his name were among a collection of Nazi papers which were being held in Israel, and a handwriting expert said that Rauca's signature on his driver's licence matched the writing on those papers.

Rauca might have been punished by the Allies in Germany soon after the end of the war, as many other members of the SS were, but he was shrewd enough to avoid getting caught. His name came up frequently during the interrogation of Germans by Allied war crimes investigators, but the authorities couldn't find him. Although they didn't realize it at the time, he was right under their noses.

He was in Germany, having retreated from Lithuania when the Nazis were pushed out by the advancing Russians in the last part of the war. He was held briefly in a prisoner camp in Germany, but then he was transferred to a military hospital, where he worked as an orderly. From there, he went to a hostel for homeless men, and then he spent about a year and a half working as a coal miner in the Ruhr Valley.

His immigration to Canada was arranged by the Canadian Christian Council for the Relief of Refugees, a joint effort of the Roman Catholic and Lutheran Churches. He landed at Saint John, N.B., aboard the *Beaverbrae*, a ship that brought some 38,000 refugees and displaced persons to Canada from the late 1940s to the mid-1950s.

How this former SS member managed to slip past Canadian immigration officers is unknown, but considering the weaknesses in the screening procedures at the time, it's not surprising that he was able to get into the country. All it took was a little creative lying on his part.

He disguised the fact that he was the "Helmut Rauka" who had served in the SS, and whose name appeared on a list of wanted war criminals, by changing the spelling of his last name from Rauka to Rauca. He also listed himself as Albert Rauca, using his real first name rather than his middle name, Helmut, which he had used in the SS.

He undoubtedly lied when he was asked if he had been in the SS. That was a routine question put to German immigrants at the time. He passed himself off as a simple German soldier, or perhaps even claimed he had been a civilian during the war years. He also likely told immigration officials that he had a farm background and that he wanted to work in the Canadian agricultural industry. This would have made him more acceptable, since Canada was short of farm laborers at the time.

The government forms which were filled out at the time of his admission could have shed light on how he got into Canada, but they were destroyed just a year or two before Rauca was arrested. Officials claimed that Rauca's records were among thousands which were considered too old to keep, and had to be disposed of because the government was running out of storage space.

Government officials said they didn't realize that these old immigration records might be needed. At best, the destruction of the records was short-sighted. At worst, it was a deliberate attempt to get rid of incriminating evidence against Rauca and other suspected war criminals who were let into Canada.

After his arrival in Canada, Rauca's first job was on a tobacco farm near Otterville, Ontario. A year later, he moved to Toronto, where he worked as a bricklayer's helper, a dishwasher, a brewery worker and a warehouse man. He was moving from job to job when war crimes investigators in East Germany somehow managed to establish that he was in Toronto. They asked the Canadian authorities to arrest him and send him to East Germany for trial, but they got no help from the Canadian government.

Rauca, like many other suspected war criminals in Canada, benefitted from the fact that an extradition request from a communist government was almost automatically turned down. The Canadian authorities were unwilling to co-operate with the communists, because the Cold War was in full swing. It had been only a decade since a major Soviet spy network had been uncovered in Canada. In 1945, a Russian embassy worker named Igor Gouzenko defected. He blew the whistle on a massive Soviet espionage operation. After that, Canada had little faith in what the Soviets said, and so when the East Germans claimed that Rauca was a war criminal, Ottawa didn't listen.

Eventually the East Germans gave up trying to get the Canadian government to extradite Rauca. They turned over their information to the West German authorities, hoping they would be able to win Canada's help. But a request from the West Germans in 1961 for Rauca's extradition also fell on deaf ears. Officials in Ottawa had quietly adopted a policy of taking no action against alleged war criminals in Canada.

The thinking at the time was that it was better to let the issue die a natural death, and at that point, with the war having been over for 15 years, that seemed like a reasonable approach. It didn't take into account the fact that many people, including the Jews of Canada, the Soviets and the West Germans were unwilling to let this happen.

Meanwhile, Rauca had run a lunchroom in Toronto and a banquet hall in Kitchener, Ontario. Then he ran a dry cleaning business. After that, he moved to Huntsville in Northern Ontario, where he spent 16 years running a motel, and where he kept pretty much to himself. He didn't become involved with the community, or socialize with his fellow motel-operators.

He was granted Canadian citizenship in 1956. His wartime activities were apparently not considered when his application was processed. He had lived a productive life since coming to Canada, and had stayed out of trouble in his new land. That was good enough to win him Canadian citizenship, despite what he had allegedly done during the war. Indeed, because of the lack of communication between government departments, it's unlikely that citizenship officials were even aware that Rauca was a suspected war criminal.

The years passed, but the West Germans didn't give up. They still wanted to prosecute Rauca. In 1970, they again asked the Canadian government to extradite Rauca, and again they got nowhere. They asked yet again in 1973, and that's when the Canadian government finally took action. It made a half-hearted effort to determine where Rauca was living, but when his name didn't turn up in a routine check of government records, Ottawa told the West Germans that the man they wanted so badly could not be located.

Meanwhile, Rauca sold his interest in the Huntsville motel and went back to Toronto, where he moved into the house of an elderly couple with whom he had become friends. He lived in that house for the next nine years, until the day he was arrested in 1982.

The arrest came about two years after the RCMP had started seriously looking for Rauca. The search began in 1980, after government policy changed to permit a more aggressive approach toward tracking down suspected war criminals whose extradition had been requested by non-communist governments.

The driving force behind this change in policy was Robert Kaplan, a Liberal MP. Kaplan was Jewish himself, and his Toronto riding of York Centre had a large Jewish population. The war criminals issue had been gradually heating up through the 1970s, and many of Kaplan's constituents were outraged at the idea that Canada was harboring Nazi war criminals. Kaplan vowed to do what he could to change the government's policy, but as a back-bench Liberal, he didn't have much clout.

He also had a formidable opponent. Pierre Trudeau, the leader of the Liberals and Prime Minister of Canada, wasn't interested in going after war criminals. Trudeau considered it a waste of effort, and felt there were many other things the government should be devoting its money and attention to. Trudeau also feared that the pursuit of war criminals would foster dissention among Canadian ethnic groups.

Kaplan wasn't content to let the matter drop. He introduced a private member's bill in 1978 calling for the automatic revoking of the Canadian citizenship of anyone who had been convicted in a foreign country of a "grave breach" of the Geneva Convention of 1949. This international agreement covered such war crimes as torturing people and killing non-combatants.

But one of the problems with Kaplan's proposal was that it could have been used to denaturalize Canadian immigrants who had been found guilty of war crimes by communist courts. The fear was that false charges, trumped up by the communists to get back at political enemies, could have been used to force the Canadian government to denaturalize them. Kaplan's bill was seen as well intentioned, but dangerous. He got no support from his Liberal colleagues, and his proposal died.

But in 1980, when the Liberals and Trudeau returned to power after the short-lived Conservative government of Joe Clark, Kaplan finally found himself in a position to do something about war criminals. Trudeau appointed him Solicitor General of Canada, in part because of growing public pressure that something be done about war criminals in Canada. Kaplan's new job included overseeing the activities of the RCMP, and that enabled him to take effective action at last on the war criminals issue.

He told the force to change its long-standing policy of not chasing after suspected war criminals in Canada, and pointed out that Rauca was still at large. The RCMP spent two years trying to find Rauca. Eventually, they learned that he had recently been issued a Canadian passport, which meant that the External Affairs Department had his address. This was supposed to be confidential information, but Kaplan got it and passed it on to the RCMP, who quickly located Rauca in north Toronto and put him under surveillance.

From that point on, the authorities proceeded cautiously. The Justice Department sent a lawyer to West Germany and Israel to determine if there was enough evidence against Rauca to make sure that a deportation application would be successful. The government didn't want to risk picking Rauca up and making a big fuss about having nabbed a suspected war criminal, only to have a judge throw the case out on the grounds that there was insufficient evidence to extradite him.

Finally, on June 17, 1982, three Mounties went to the house where Rauca lived. They arrested the 73-year-old man on charges of aiding and abetting the murder of 10,500 Lithuanians in 1941.

The arrest caused a sensation across Canada, particularly within the Jewish community. Rauca was the first Canadian ever to be charged with committing war crimes, and his arrest made front-page headlines.

He remained in custody, at least partly for his own safety, for several months. During his dragged-out extradition hearing, dozens of members of the Jewish Defence League marched on the sidewalk outside the courtroom wearing T-shirts which read "Never Again."

Rauca didn't testify or call witnesses to try and prove his innocence, but in a letter he wrote in his jail cell, he said:

> I have read newspaper accounts of the proceedings against me and I see that it has never been made clear that I have said and say now that I am not guilty of such murder or murders while I served in the forces of the Third Reich or at any time.

During the court proceedings, his lawyer argued that Rauca was entitled to remain in Canada under the new Charter of Rights and Freedoms, which had recently come into effect. If that tactic had worked, it could have tied up the case in court for years, but Chief

Justice Gregory Evans of the Ontario Supreme Court ruled that a person's constitutional rights in Canada were not absolute.

The judge cited the section of the Charter which said that individual rights are subject to "reasonable limits prescribed by law as can be demonstrably justified in a free and democratic society." On that basis, he ordered that Rauca be sent to West Germany to stand trial.

He was extradited in May 1983, but five months later, before he could be put on trial, Rauca died of cancer in a Frankfurt prison hospital.

CHAPTER 15

The Americans Lead the Way

The United States, like Canada, accepted war criminals as immigrants after the war, and like Canada, the U.S. did almost nothing about them for decades. But this began to change in the early 1970s, and by the end of the decade the U.S. government was in full pursuit of alleged war criminals in the United States.

The American news media played a big role in raising public awareness. Hermine Braunsteiner Ryan's legal case (see Chapter 10) got big play, especially when she was deported to West Germany in 1973. There were many news stories about suspected war criminals in various other parts of the United States. Public sentiment gradually shifted from indifference to interest in the subject, and then to concern that nothing was being done about the problem.

Pressure for action increased as the public learned more details about the Holocaust. The 1970s was a time of new interest in this grim aspect of the history of the Second World War. Some people said it took so long for people to pay attention to this painful subject because post-traumatic shock had set in after the war. Denial of the Holocaust had been a psychological defence mechanism.

People didn't have to deal with guilt and horror, if they didn't think about what happened to the Jews. According to this theory, a fair amount of time had to pass before people were able to accept the reality of this massive assault on humanity. By the 1970s, more than a generation had passed, and that was long enough.

In 1978, NBC Television broadcast a four-part mini-series titled "Holocaust" which vividly showed what happened to the Jews during the war. The series contained shocking scenes which had a profound effect on younger viewers, most of whom previously knew little about the Holocaust. Thanks to television dramatics, the murder of the Jews became a real event to them, just as it did to still another generation of young people in the 1990s when the movie called *Schindler's List* was produced.

American Jewish organizations worked to raise public awareness of the war criminals problem and to put pressure on the U.S. government to take action. One of the most successful of these groups had a Canadian connection. It was the Friends of Simon Wiesenthal Centre for Holocaust Studies, which was started in Los Angeles in 1977 by Marvin Hier, a rabbi who began his career in Vancouver.

Hier was trained in New York and then went to Vancouver in the early 1960s to lead the city's orthodox Jewish community. A charismatic figure and a community activist, Hier "was born with the soul of an activist," according to an article which appeared years later in the *Los Angeles Times Magazine*. "Since he was a child," the article said, "he dreamed of taking revenge upon the Nazis who wiped out most of his parents' families in Poland. For Hier – as for most Jews – the Holocaust was the searing event of the 20th century."

Rabbi Hier led a demonstration against Alexei Kosygin when the Soviet Prime Minister visited Vancouver in 1975. Dressed in prayer shawls, Heir and his followers greeted Kosygin with loud prayers for the oppressed Jews of the Soviet Union. Two years later, he moved to Los Angeles and started the Wiesenthal Centre.

The centre was named after the world-famous Nazi hunter, and was the American equivalent of Yad Vashem, the Israeli national Holocaust museum in Jerusalem. But the Wiesenthal Centre was more than just a place for old photographs and files. Hier used it as the focus of his political activism, and turned it into one of the loudest voices calling for the prosecution of Nazi war criminals in the United States.

Two Jewish members of the United States House of Representatives, Joshua Eilberg and Elizabeth Holtzman, lobbied their colleagues to win support for a law which would enable the U.S. Justice Department to go after war criminals. Until then, the task had been the responsibility of the U.S. Naturalization and Immigration Service, which did virtually nothing in this regard.

In 1979, the new law was enacted by Congress and signed by President Jimmy Carter. It provided funding of about $3-million a year for a 50-member war crimes unit within the Justice Department, devoted to tracking down suspected Nazi war criminals and taking them to court. Interestingly, the Canadian Justice Department's war crimes unit ended up with the same-size budget and staff after it was established, eight years later.

The new American prosecution unit was called the Office of Special Investigations, or the OSI. Skeptics said that launching a hunt for Nazi war criminals so long after the end of the war was a waste of time and money, but right from the start it was successful. It found all kinds of ex-Nazis and Nazi collaborators living in the U.S.A. By 1985, just as the Deschênes commission on war criminals was getting under way in Canada, the OSI had taken 45 suspects to court and succeeded in deporting six of them.

The OSI began its task by digging through old Nazi documents and U.S. immigration files, and by inviting the general public to submit tips. A flood of names poured in. Many of these allegations were groundless, but in cases in which the investigators turned up substantial evidence, the suspect was quietly offered an opportunity to respond before legal action was undertaken.

The OSI had a powerful legal weapon. The Displaced Persons Act, which governed the admission of immigrants to the United States, prohibited anyone from entering the country who had been a Nazi or assisted the Nazis. This gave the OSI the lever it needed to take war criminals to court.

If the OSI could show that a suspect had lied about his Nazi past when he entered the States, the suspect could be deported. Taking the suspect before a deportation hearing, rather than a criminal court, gave the OSI a big advantage. The standard of proof needed to establish guilt in a deportation case was lower.

In a deportation case, the OSI had only to prove that the suspect "likely" lied about his past. To prove guilt in a criminal case, the standard of proof was higher. In a criminal court, guilt had to be established beyond a reasonable doubt.

If the immigrant had already obtained U.S. citizenship – and many of them had – the OSI had to strip him of his citizenship before he could be deported. But that, too, could be done fairly easily, using a legal procedure known as denaturalization. The immigrant could be denaturalized if it could be proven that he had obtained his citizenship illegally.

Since one of the requirements for obtaining U.S. citizenship was that the applicant must have been in the United States legally at the time he was naturalized, the same evidence used in the deportation hearing could be used in the denaturalization hearing.

If he was a war criminal, then he had entered the country illegally. If he was illegally in the country, then he had obtained his citizenship illegally, and he could be denaturalized. This technique was commonly known as the denaturalization and deportation method, or the D and D procedure.

D and D worked well until the last step, but then there was often a problem. After a deportation order had been issued, the Americans had to find a suitable foreign country willing to accept the suspected war criminal. Many of the war criminals were from Eastern Europe, and the Americans didn't consider these countries to be acceptable deportation destinations. While they wanted to get rid of their war criminals, the Americans weren't willing to throw their outcasts to the communist wolves.

D and D proceedings were often drawn-out affairs, enabling suspected war criminals to remain in the United States for many years while their cases dragged through the courts. Valerian Trifa was a classic example. He was the archbishop of the Romanian Orthodox Episcopacy in the United States. During the war, Trifa had been a leader of the Iron Guard in Romania, and was allegedly responsible for the deaths of many innocent people.

The U.S. government began denaturalization proceedings against Trifa in 1975. Five years later, he consented to giving up his own citizenship to avoid having evidence of his Nazi crimes filed with the court. Then he turned around and appealed from his own denaturalization consent decree, dragging out the case for another few years. He employed similar tactics to stave off deportation, and continued to live in luxury on his church's grand estate in Grass Lake, Michigan.

The U.S. government kept after him, and in 1984 Trifa voluntarily moved to Portugal, where he continued to enjoy a pleasant life. He had used clever legal tactics to delay his departure from the United States for nine years.

Allan A. Ryan Jr., who was the director of the OSI for most of its first five years, maintained that it was the principle rather than the outcome which was important when it came to prosecuting war criminals. Ryan said that stripping them of their American citizenship was a severe punishment in itself, even if the war criminals remained in the United States.

Ryan saw denaturalization as the civil equivalent of religious excommunication. He theorized that war criminals should hang their heads in shame because they had been rejected by their fellow-citizens. But the people who suffered this "punishment" laughed at that. The only hardships they suffered were not being able to get a U.S. passport, and not being permitted to vote in elections.

Canadians who were interested in dealing with war criminals in their own country watched the OSI's successes and failures with interest. Some of them felt that Canada should follow the American lead and use the D and D procedure.

Others were in favor of a so-called made-in-Canada solution. They thought it would be better to bring suspects up on criminal charges in Canadian courts. That way, those who were convicted could be sent to Canadian prisons. But as long as Pierre Trudeau and the Liberals were in power, that was not going to happen. The Liberals had no intention of amending the Criminal Code so that suspected war criminals could be tried in Canada.

Things changed, however, in 1984, when Trudeau retired. John Turner, the new Prime Minister, called an election and was soundly trounced by Brian Mulroney and the Progressive Conservatives. Mulroney was a great admirer of the United States. He was more receptive to the idea that Canada should follow the American lead when it came to taking some sort of action against war criminals.

Within a few months of Mulroney's election, an opportunity came along which enabled him to set the wheels in motion.

CHAPTER 16

Mengele in Canada?

Sol Littman caused a sensation early in 1985. He announced at a news conference in Toronto that Dr. Josef Mengele, the world's most notorious surviving Nazi war criminal, had applied for admission to Canada in the early 1960s.

Littman, the Canadian representative of the Simon Wiesenthal Centre, said it was not only possible that Mengele had come to Canada at that time, but that he might still be in the country. It was a stunning suggestion, and it caught the attention of both the Canadian public and the new Conservative government.

Immigration Department officials scurried to check their records, to see if what Littman was saying might be true. No record of Mengele's entry into Canada could be found, but an old Ontario Provincial Police report indicated that a man who might have been Mengele was living on a farm in southern Ontario in the early 1960s.

Acting on a tip from a citizen, the OPP had conducted a slow and quiet investigation which was dropped when the suspect disappeared. It was clear from the police records that the OPP didn't want to pick up a suspect whose case would have been a potential hot potato, and so it had dragged its heels for months. This suggested that Mengele might have slipped away while the police diddled around.

If he was still in Canada, what could be done about it? Lawyers pored over the Criminal Code and other statutes to determine what charges, if any, could be laid. Meanwhile, ordinary Canadians, fascinated by the highly publicized case after Littman's announcement, started wondering if the old German living down street might be the world's most-wanted war criminal.

Mengele's possible presence in Canada caught the public's interest as no other war crimes story had done since the trial of Kurt Meyer in 1945 (see Chapters 1-2). Mengele was not just another suspected war criminal. He was not just one of the many who had popped up over the years in Canadian media reports. Mengele was a "somebody." He was a superstar of villainy, a cold-blooded killer with a price on his head. Foreign governments were offering millions of dollars for his capture. He was the big prize in an international monster contest, and here was Sol Littman saying that he might be right here in Canada.

The Israelis would have loved to have gotten their hands on him. They would likely have tried him, the same way they tried Adolf Eichmann after they kidnapped him in Brazil in 1960. The West Germans were also after Mengele, eager to demonstrate that they were still serious about punishing old Nazis. The American wanted him too, but what they would have done with him is uncertain, in view of the fact that he was never known to have entered the United States or to have committed crimes against American laws.

Canadians already knew a lot about Mengele, and had seen his picture many times on TV and in the newspapers. They had even seen him in the movies. Gregory Peck played a doctor much like him in *The Boys from Brazil*, a story about a Nazi physician who created a batch of Hitler clones in a test tube. The real-life Mengele was even more horrible than the one Gregory Peck portrayed so well on the screen.

As the chief physician at the Auschwitz concentration camp in Poland during the war, Mengele had performed sadistic medical experiments. He had poured acid in the eyes of babies, and thrown men into tanks of ice water to see how long they could last.

He was nicknamed the Angel of Death because he had walked through groups of Jews indicating with the touch of his hand who should live and who should die. Mengele had also personally dropped Zyklon B into the gas chambers, and laughed as his Jewish victims clawed at the locked doors and finally dropped to the floor.

Mengele in Canada?

It was a stunning suggestion, but everyone knew it was not impossible. Not only were there those old stories about other suspected war criminals said to be living in Canada. There was also the fact that the source of the allegation was generally considered to be Canada's leading expert on the subject of war criminals. Littman was a respected journalist who had written for Canada's largest daily newspaper, *The Toronto Star*, and had reported for CBC television.

His reputation had been further enhanced by a book he had recently written about the Albert Rauca case. At the time it was published in 1983, it was the only book of any significance on the subject of war criminals in Canada. In his book, Littman told Canadians how Rauca had managed to get into Canada with no difficulty, and how he had lived in the country for 32 years before he was arrested by the RCMP.

Now Littman was talking about a far bigger Nazi killer than Rauca, another monster who might also have found safe haven in Canada. If anyone else had made the claim, it might have seemed far-fetched, but Littman was a man who knew what he was talking about – or so it seemed.

As well as being an author and journalist, he was a Second World War veteran and a scholar. He had served in the Canadian Army during the war, and gone on to earn a master's degree in sociology.

He had studied the Holocaust, learning as much as he could about the destruction of six million European Jews. It was a subject which caught his attention rather late in his life. He felt that it had not happened earlier because he, like a lot of other Jews, had initially tried to put it out of his mind because it was so horrible, but it kept coming back, bothering him.

He compared it to having a pebble in his shoe. He found that he could ignore it and keep walking for only so long. Eventually, he had to stop and do something about it.

Littman read everything he could find about the Holocaust, and then travelled across Europe, doing original research by digging through archives. Finally, he came to the conclusion that as many as 6,000 Nazi war criminals had made their way into Canada, and that in the mid-1980s, about half of them were still alive. Soon after that, he had been hired by the Simon Wiesenthal Centre to establish a Canadian office in Toronto.

And so when he spoke out about Mengele, he had a lot of credibility.

After writing a letter to Brian Mulroney setting out his suspicions about Mengele, and getting no reply from the Prime Minister, Littman called a news conference. He announced that the

Wiesenthal Centre had obtained U.S. government documents showing that Mengele might have entered Canada 23 years earlier.

Most Nazi hunters, including Simon Wiesenthal himself, had believed that Mengele was hiding in South America, but Littman said that the recently obtained documents showed that Mengele had applied for a visa to immigrate to Canada.

Littman came to his conclusion on the basis of a dozen documents which had been obtained by the Wiesenthal Centre from the U.S. government under the Freedom of Information Act. He said that he had only some of the relevant documents, and that an application had been submitted for the rest, but he felt he already could conclude that Mengele had applied to the Canadian embassy in Buenos Aires for admission to Canada as a landed immigrant in late May or early June of 1962.

Littman said he was certain that Mengele had applied to come to Canada, that it was "possible" that Mengele had actually been admitted to Canada, and that he "might" still be here.

As things turned out, these were shaky conclusions, based on too little evidence. Littman had jumped the gun, and spoken out before he had enough information. But when he made his big announcement, he didn't hedge. He said there was "no doubt" that Mengele had applied to come to Canada. Having reached this conclusion, Littman took his shaky reasoning further. "These factors," he asserted, "make it impossible to rule out the possibility – incredible as it may seem – that Mengele was knowingly admitted to Canada."

Then he clinched it with his most astounding claim. "This leaves us," he concluded, "with the frightening possibility that Mengele may actually be living in Canada today."

It was hot stuff, and it got big play in the media. It was also well timed. The Mulroney government was looking for ways to set itself apart from the previous Liberal regime. For years, the Liberals had been tap-dancing around the war criminals issue, and Jewish groups had been complaining about it. And now here was Littman, conveniently providing the Tories with an opportunity to take action on the war crimes issue, if that's what they wanted to do.

Meanwhile, other events were unfolding. Ernst Zundel was on trial in Toronto for "spreading false news likely to cause injury or mischief to the public interest." Zundel was brought up on the charges after he claimed that the Holocaust was a hoax.

The government was also preparing to go to trial against James Keegstra. He was charged with "willfully promoting hatred against an identifiable group" after telling his students in high school history classes that the Holocaust was a lie, told as part of an international Jewish conspiracy.

These cases were bringing the Holocaust before the public on an almost daily basis, and this helped to create a climate of interest when Littman raised the possibility of Mengele's presence in Canada.

Interest was further heightened because many news reports were also being published at the same time about Klaus Barbie, the German SS officer who had headed the Gestapo in Lyon, France, and who had been the boss of Jacques de Bernonville, who had come to Quebec in 1947 (see Chapter 6). After the war, the United States government had employed Barbie as an intelligence agent, then helped him escape to Bolivia.

Had Canada been involved in this seedy business? Had Mengele been given a new identity and a new life in Canada in exchange for Cold War espionage services? These were questions which needed answering.

The news media picked up where Littman left off, reporting that the RCMP was deliberately covering up information about war criminals in Canada. Editorials blasted the government for the fact that Canadians had to learn about Mengele's Canadian connections from documents released by the Americans. They demanded that the Canadian government stop keeping secrets from the Canadian people and open up the files.

In February, the Mulroney government finally decided to act. It was a pivotal moment in the history of the war crimes issue in Canada.

The government appointed Quebec Superior Court Judge Jules Deschênes to conduct an inquiry into the "Mengele Affair," as it was soon dubbed. But the government didn't stop there. It asked Deschênes to go much further, and look into the whole subject of war criminals in Canada. It asked the judge to find out how many war criminals were living in the country, and to come up with suggestions on how to deal with them.

As things turned out, these assignments were far more important than the first one. The Mengele Affair soon fizzled.

Deschênes discovered that Mengele wasn't in Canada, and had never been in Canada. In fact, he had not even applied to come to

Canada. The whole thing had been a pile of misinterpretations and misunderstandings, a hornet's nest stirred up by Sol Littman. Deschênes found that Littman had read far more into those U.S. government documents than he should have.

The truth was that in 1962, a citizen had reported to the Ontario Provincial Police that a German immigrant living on a farm in southern Ontario looked something like Mengele. The RCMP and the Department of External Affairs were called into the case.

A routine inquiry was made in West Germany, where the U.S. Army kept lists of suspected war criminals. It was this routine inquiry which put Mengele's name into the records that had been obtained by the Wiesenthal Centre.

Deschênes found that the facts had been blown out of all proportion. Littman had turned a fruitless inquiry on the German farmer into an immigration application which had supposedly been made by Josef Mengele from Argentina.

Littman tried to explain what had happened. He said that he had combined a few facts which he had gleaned from the U.S. government documents with his background knowledge of the way the immigration system worked, and had come up with what he thought was a "possible scenario" of what "might" have occurred.

He ultimately acknowledged that he had acted "somewhat hastily."

Littman's boss, Rabbi Marvin Hier, the head of the Wiesenthal Centre's operations in Los Angeles, tried to put the best face on the matter. Hier said that government secrecy had prevented Littman from having access to enough information to determine the truth about the Mengele Affair, so Littman had been forced to do the best he could with the limited amount of information available to him.

He tried to turn criticism of Littman into an attack on the government for not looking hard enough for war criminals, and for not making public the information that it did have.

"It just shows you," Hier concluded, "that without the resources of the major intelligence agencies and governments involved, that's what happens."

Others took a harsher view.

Spokesmen for the Canadian Jewish Congress and B'Nai Brith issued statements disassociating themselves from Littman. They gave him no credit for finally getting the government to take action on the war criminals issue, although they had been trying to do the same thing themselves for years, without success.

Instead, they complained about the way Littman had done what they couldn't do, and criticized the way the inquiry was going to be run. They called Littman a "loose cannon," but failed to acknowledge that they had been firing shots for years without getting the government to budge.

Ivan Whitehall, a Justice Department lawyer working with the Deschênes commission, went so far as to brand Littman as a "vigilante." Whitehall accused Littman of using the Mengele case to pressure the government into conducting an unnecessary and expensive public inquiry.

Once the Deschênes investigation got under way, the Mengele Affair quickly receded into the background. But if anyone deserves credit for the establishment of the commission, it is Sol Littman. Almost single-handedly, he finally got the government to do something about the persistent "pebble in Canada's shoe. "

CHAPTER 17

Twenty Top Suspects

The taxpayers laid out a lot of money for what was supposed to be have been a full-scale inquiry into war criminals in Canada. The people who picked up the $4-million tab didn't get their money's worth.

This wasn't surprising. Ottawa had spent decades concealing what it had done and not done with respect to war criminals, so it was unlikely that a government-appointed commissioner would finally tell the Canadian people the truth. The commissioner, Mr. Justice Jules Deschênes, should have provided the public with detailed and specific answers to the key questions about alleged war criminals in Canada: How many of them were there? How did they get into the country? How many were still alive? How had they spent their lives since coming to Canada? What were they doing now? Were they in fact guilty? And if they were, what should be done about them?

These were the main questions, but instead of answers, Deschênes gave the taxpayers a 1,000-page report which was a masterpiece of bafflegab and useless information. It contained so little of substance that it should have been titled "Massive Volume Covering Up War Crimes Secrets."

That's what the public got, but the government got something better. It got a private report from the judge containing detailed information on 20 men identified as being prime suspects.

The names of those 20 men and the information about them in that secret report have never been made public, but Deschênes urged the government to take legal action against them right away.

But that just didn't happen. The government dragged its feet.

Meanwhile, the clock was still ticking, and time was running out. That had been the name of Ottawa's game all along. The government knew that this was one problem that could be fixed by stonewalling, but Deschênes hadn't been accommodating in that regard. He had told the government that these cases required "urgent attention," thus putting the government on the spot.

Speed was essential, he pointed out, because all of the suspects were elderly. It was going to be a race against the biological clock to take legal action against them before they became too old or ill to stand the stress of a trial, and before those who could testify against them faded into history.

Who were these 20 old men?

Nobody knew, except for Deschênes, his investigators, and the handful of government insiders who had access to his secret report. Deschênes kept all the details about them out of his public report. He said that he felt obligated to protect their privacy, giving no weight to the fact that the public might have a right to know their identities, particularly since he had concluded that there was a considerable amount of evidence against them. He simply turned over the information to the Justice Department, and urged swift government action.

As we will see in upcoming chapters, the government took legal action against only five alleged war criminals over the course of the next five years. Whether or not those five were among the 20 cited by Deschênes has never been revealed. But even if all five were on the list, then 15 of the 20 cases identified by Deschênes as requiring "urgent attention" were not taken to court.

The Justice Department has never explained why it did not pursue these cases, despite the fact that a special unit within the Justice Department was established to prosecute war criminals. Whenever officials of that unit have been asked what happened to the 20 suspects cited by Deschênes, they have hidden behind the excuse that this is "confidential information."

While the authorities mulled over the report and tried to decide what to do about the 20 suspects, Deschênes presented the public with a massive report that fell far short of informing Canadians about what was really going on in their country with respect to war criminals.

Deschênes spend almost two years carrying out his mission. He hired a staff of about 50 lawyers, former police officers, historians, administrators and others to assist him. Deschênes and his team spent the better part of 1985 and 1986 travelling across Canada, holding hearings and taking evidence.

The public sessions produced mainly hot air. Special interests and ethnic groups saw the inquiry as an opportunity to score points against each other. People frequently turned up at public sessions and tried to give speeches berating their opponents.

There was also a lot of bickering between lawyers representing the Justice Department, Ukrainian-Canadians and Jewish organizations. They travelled around with the commission, making sure that their interests were protected. The in-fighting between them was so bad that when the commission was sitting in Winnipeg, Deschênes had to remind the antagonists that the inquiry wasn't being held just so they could fight the Second World War all over again.

The judge conducted all the most revealing commission sessions in private. That's when he heard from suspects who were summoned to appear before him, as well as from people who had evidence to offer against suspected war criminals. These "in camera" sessions were always held behind closed doors, and the records of the proceedings have been kept private.

Deschênes' findings and recommendations, which he turned over to the government at the end of 1986, were released to the public three months later in a sanitized form, with all the details about individual suspects carefully removed.

The report was inadequate as far as informing the public was concerned, but it was greeted with approval and relief by the various special interest groups. The Jews were happy because the judge had confirmed that they weren't dreaming when they said that a lot of Nazi war criminals had come to Canada, and that many of them were still around. The Ukrainians were happy because Deschênes had concluded that they weren't all war criminals – not even the ones who had served in the SS Galicia Division (see Chapter 7).

The federal government was happiest of all, because Deschênes had not come down hard on the authorities for letting so many war criminals into the country in the first place, and for doing almost nothing about them for decades. Deschênes pleased the Mulroney government, which had appointed him, by providing the Conservatives with such a huge pile of information that he created the illusion that a thorough study had been carried out. This made the Tories look good.

But the judge also served up such a bewildering array of options on how the government might proceed that the Conservatives were able to continue to do nothing, as their predecessors had, at least for awhile. Deschênes had already been good for a couple of years' delay. While the commission was still at work, the government could say that it had to await the judge's findings.

Now that the government finally had the judge's report, it could say they it was carefully examining the findings and the various options which Deschênes had presented before deciding what to do next.

In the public part of his report, Deschênes waded through the details of the hundreds of cases which he felt were not worth proceeding with. He discussed each of these cases at length, seemingly intent on making the point that the vast majority of suspected war criminals were not war criminals at all. But he discussed these cases in such general terms that it was impossible to determine who he was talking about, or what these non-suspects had allegedly done or not done.

In a typical example, the judge referred to one man as having lived in "an Eastern European country" during the war, and then went on to talk about when the man had come to Canada, when he had obtained his citizenship and so forth. Then the judge said that since no evidence had been found that the man had committed war crimes, his file should be closed. The judge gave no details on what efforts had been made to find evidence against the man. Instead, the judge simply wrote the case off on the basis that there was insufficient evidence.

Deschênes plodded on in this fashion through case after case, repeating himself over and over, using whole paragraphs of similarly-worded text for one suspect after another. It looked like he was trying to fill space and to demonstrate how thorough the investigation had been, but Deschênes might easily have accomplished the same thing by simply listing all the cases that fell into the same general pattern, and then explaining why all of those files should be closed.

The judge put little emphasis on the fact that the commission's staff of 50 included only four investigators – all retired police officers. He also didn't stress that it was no wonder these investigators found so little, since they spent the majority of their time making routine inquiries of government departments to collect such non-incriminating information as the name of the ship on which the suspect had come to Canada, and whether or not he had applied for a Canadian passport.

Deschênes was so caught up in discussing individual cases that he failed to give generalized information in a clear and pertinent manner. For example, he didn't even provide a good estimate of how many war criminals had come to Canada, and how many were still living in the country.

And his explanation of how they got into the country was so convoluted and full of references to government regulations and the like that he failed to make clear a key point – that the government didn't try very hard to keep suspected war criminals out, and that's why they had an easy time getting into Canada.

The report was incredibly confusing when the judge started tossing around numbers. He added up and subdivided the figures in so many different ways that it was virtually impossible to figure out what he was talking about.

In laborious detail, Deschênes explained that he had been provided with various lists of suspects which had been submitted to him from many different sources – everyone from Simon Wiesenthal in Vienna to the RCMP and private citizens, as well as several Jewish groups. He then went on to ridicule some of the people who had provided him with information, suggesting that they had deliberately inflated their figures in order to make the problem look worse than it was.

He explained how he had built a "master list" of 774 names from various lists which had been given to him. But when 38 more names arrived near the end of the research phase of his investigation, he didn't just add to the total. He created a second list, which he called the "addendum." Then, for some reason, he came up with still a third list, which consisted of another 71 names.

So there were three Deschênes lists, and together they contained the names of 883 suspects. Sometimes Deschênes would make calculations based on that total of 883, but often he would take only part of the total and use it as his base number. He then would subdivide the figure in various ways, breaking it down this way and that way with no apparent purpose.

Frequently, his numbers just didn't add up. For instance, at the start of his report, he talked about the 822 opinions he had written on individual cases, but then he went on to reveal that the total number of suspects on his three lists was 883. Why had he written only 822 opinions? What happened to the other 61 suspects? He didn't say.

But as he went on and on in his report, a pattern emerged. He kept whittling down the lists, eliminating people who were already dead, who had left Canada and so forth. He chopped off more people who could not be found, or who couldn't possibly be war criminals because of their age or some other factor. Then he culled out many more because his small team of investigators had found no evidence against them.

Eventually Deschênes reduced the total to 29 prime suspects. These were people, he said, against whom a substantial amount of evidence had been found. But then he chopped nine of them off the list, and finally came up with the 20 prime suspects whose files he turned over to the Justice Department with a view toward swift prosecution. What about the other nine?

Once again, Deschênes withheld vital information from the public. He said that in his opinion, these nine people should be left alone so that they could "finish their days in peace." Why? Deschênes didn't say. Presumably they were too old or ill to prosecute, but he offered no explanation, and so Canadians were left to guess.

As for the remaining 20 – the prime suspects that Deschênes said required "urgent attention" – he had two proposals on how they could be dealt with. He said they could either be stripped of their citizenship and deported, or they could be put on trial in Canadian courts.

But if the latter course was going to be followed, Deschênes pointed out, the government would have to amend the Criminal Code to make such prosecutions possible. And that, of course, would require time.

Meanwhile, the clock was ticking.

CHAPTER 18

The Made-In-Canada Solution

Jules Deschênes said that ideally, suspects should be sent back to Europe to be tried where their alleged crimes had been committed, but this wasn't always possible. In such cases, he suggested, suspected war criminals living in Canada should be brought before Canadian courts and put on trial here.

Deschênes urged the government to move quickly on this, while there was still time to act. He knew that the 20 prime suspects he had identified were already old, and that the longer the government delayed in prosecuting them, the less likely it would be that they would be brought to justice.

Deschênes suggested that the government amend the Criminal Code to legalize domestic prosecution, but this would be unusual legislation, for two reasons. It would be extra-territorial, and it would be retroactive.

"Extra-territorial" meant that the suspects would be tried in Canada for crimes allegedly committed outside Canada. Normally, a country's courts have jurisdiction only in cases where offences are committed within the territorial boundaries of that country, but there are exceptions.

For instance, people who commit crimes at sea involving Canadian ships can be tried in Canadian courts. Canadian public servants who commit offences abroad can also be tried in Canadian courts.

The law covering these and similar extra-territorial offences is set out in Section 6 of the Criminal Code of Canada, and it was this section which Deschênes recommended be amended to include war criminals. He felt that this was an appropriate place for a new law which would criminalize activities that had been carried out in Europe during the war.

But Deschênes said the law should be broad enough to cover other war crimes, no matter when or where they had been committed. This would enable the authorities to use the new law against people who had committed war crimes in other places and in other times.

The second special thing about Deschênes' proposal was that the war crimes law would be retroactive. That was a greater problem than simply making it extra-territorial. Retroactive legislation makes a given action a crime after it has already been committed. Such legislation went against centuries of legal tradition, and struck at the heart of the concept that a person is innocent of a crime until proven guilty.

Yet when it came to dealing with war criminals, it, too, was not unprecedented. The idea of retroactivity had been used by the Allies when they put the surviving top Nazis at Nuremberg after the war. They nabbed the Nazis and then proclaimed laws to punish them. The Canadians had done the same thing themselves when they passed the retroactive military regulations which were used to try Kurt Meyer and the six other German war criminals in 1945 and 1946 (see Chapters 1-3).

In principle, retroactive legislation has a serious problem. It is viewed by many legal scholars as fundamentally unfair, because it criminalizes behavior after the fact – that is, retroactively.

For example, suppose a man is crossing a bridge, looks down and sees a person drowning in a river. Even though there's a lifebuoy nearby that the man could toss to save the drowning victim, he fails to throw it. He just stands there and watches the man drown. Maybe he doesn't want to get involved, or maybe he's never seen a person drown before and he wonders what it will be like. For whatever reason, he just stands and watches.

He may be morally reprehensible, but he's within his legal rights, because it's not a crime for a person to stand and watch another person drown. The man is under no legal obligation to toss the lifebuoy. He may be a deplorable human being, but he's not a criminal, at least not according to the law.

But then suppose the government comes along, years later, and decides that people should be required to help one another under such circumstances. The government passes a law which makes it a crime to just stand and watch a drowning. The new law means that from now on, a man, if he is able to do so, must throw a lifebuoy to a drowning person. Anyone who fails to do so, from that date forward, is guilty of a crime.

Fair enough. But what about the man who failed to throw the lifebuoy, years before? Can he now be punished for committing a crime? If the law is made retroactive, then he can. If the law is retroactive, it says that the man should have thrown the lifebuoy, and that he can be now be punished for failing to throw it, away back when.

Is such a law unjust, because it criminalizes behavior retroactively? Does it open the door for the government to pass similar laws? Does it makes it possible for the government to "get" people for a lot of things which happened in the past, and which weren't crimes when they happened?

That is what an assortment of dictators have done over the years. They have passed retroactive laws to "get" their opponents for things they've done in the past. It's a standard technique, used by totalitarian regimes to nominally legalize the abuse of human rights.

Traditionally, a person can only be charged with committing a crime if what he has done has already been declared to be against the law when he does it. For many years, this has been a basic principle of justice, and it has been an essential safeguard to guarantee the protection of individual rights.

In the United States, where individual rights are protected by the Constitution more strongly than they are in Canada, an attempt to try war criminals extra-territorially and retroactively would have been illegal. That's why the Americans have never used it. Instead, they have relied on denaturalization and deportation procedures.

But Deschênes proposed to do things a different way in Canada. As a Quebec Superior Court judge and a legal scholar with an international reputation, he was sure that under the Canadian Constitution, his solution would be legal.

Deschênes thought it was all right to pass retroactive legislation to deal with war criminals, because what they had done was clearly wrong at the time they had done it. Here's how he explained it in his report:

> We are not aiming to make acts, which were deemed innocent when committed, criminal now; such would be unacceptable retroactivity. But extermination of a civilian population, for instance, was already as much criminal in 1940 as it would be today, under the laws of all so-called civilized nations. We are only trying to establish now in Canada a forum where those suspected of having committed such offences may be tried, if found in Canada.

Deschênes' proposal to try war criminals in Canadian courts was greeted with widespread approval by those who had been urging for years that something be done to deal with the problem of war criminals in Canada. Few people objected on the grounds that retroactive legislation went against basic legal principles. Fewer still were worried about whether the new legislation would work or not.

It seemed like such a splendid idea that even the federal government, under a lot of pressure to do something about war criminals, rushed to embrace the made-in-Canada solution. With unusual speed, the new law was passed by Parliament. In September 1987, just six months after the Deschênes report was made public, the Criminal Code was amended.

This set the stage for the arrest of the first suspect, Imre Finta, before the year was out.

Finta was very likely one of the 20 prime suspects identified by Deschênes as requiring urgent attention. At the time of his arrest, people who were keen to see suspected war criminals tried in Canadian courts rejoiced. They thought that it was the start of a legal process which they felt was a long time in coming. They thought the made-in-Canada solution was ideal for prosecuting people like Finta.

But if they had been able to see what lay ahead in the Finta case and other cases to follow, they would not have been so optimistic. In hindsight, we can now see that they would have been well advised to consider more carefully the words of caution expressed by those who were not so infatuated by the made-in-Canada solution.

They might even have gone back to the early 1950s, when Major-General E.L.M. Burns, one of Canada's most distinguished soldiers, warned against bringing suspected war criminals before courts in democratic countries. Burns was discussing the question of whether losing generals should be hanged for war crimes, but what he said applied to people of all ranks. Writing in *Saturday Night* magazine, this is what General Burns said:

> Experience in dealing with war criminals after World War I had shown that if they are given the protection of the legal procedure in force in any civilized non-communist country, it is very difficult to secure a conviction. Legally valid evidence is very hard to get.

Those words applied to privates and corporals as well as generals, and they were even more true in the late 1980s than they were in the early 1950s. By the late 1980s, thanks to many pro-defendant court decisions, and thanks also to the Canadian Constitution, which went into effect in 1982, accused people in Canada had acquired more legal rights.

This made it even harder to secure a conviction against suspected war criminals, as subsequent events were to show.

CHAPTER 19

Ottawa's Dirty Little Secrets

Suspected war criminals were let into Canada as a reward for helping U.S. and British intelligence agencies, according to an Ottawa historian named Alti Rodal.

Rodal worked as a researcher for the Deschênes commission. She had access to secret government documents and interviewed civil servants who told her things they wouldn't say publicly. Rodal produced a 540-page report, but you can't walk into a public library and pick up a copy.

The government has never published this report, even though Deschênes himself recommended that it be widely circulated. You have to apply for it under the federal Access to Information Act. Even then, you only get a chopped-up version, full of deletions and omissions, ostensibly made to protect people's privacy and preserve national security.

Still, there's enough left by the censors to show that suspected war criminals were deliberately let into Canada after they helped Allied spy agencies do battle against the communists in the post-war years.

At the very least, the authorities in Ottawa let themselves be used by these agencies, and closed their eyes when suspected war criminals were slipped into Canada under false names. Canadian officials might even have been directly involved in clandestine operations which resulted in unsavory characters settling in Canada. Rodal says the evidence she obtained was inconclusive on this score, and further research is needed.

People who worked for the Nazis were useful to the West after the war. They had detailed knowledge about the communists, and the Allies took advantage of their expertise. Atrocities such people may have committed during the war were overlooked. Post-war spy agencies felt that the old war was over and the new war – the Cold War against the communists – had begun.

Rodal says that British intelligence had long-standing pre-war links with various nationalistic groups in Eastern Europe which collaborated with the Nazis, especially against the Soviets. She concludes:

> It would be reasonable to assume . . . that British intelligence services resumed their links with such former agents after the war, and then played an important part in their resettlement.

She also concludes that it would have been easier for the British than for the Americans to slip war criminals into Canada.

> Given that Britain used former Nazis and Nazi collaborators for intelligence purposes, and given the central role British intelligence played in making checks for Canadian screening officers on prospective immigrants to Canada – in some cases taking charge of the entire screening procedure on behalf of Canadian authorities – there was certainly scope for the British to help provide resettlement opportunities in Canada for former Nazis and Nazi collaborators.

> It may be assumed, too, that given Canada's special relationship with Britain, British officials carried weight and influence with Canadian authorities, particularly in matters relating to the alliance against the threat of Communism. It is most improbable, however, that either the British or Canadian government would willingly disclose, even after forty years, information bearing out such allegations.

Not all of the suspected war criminals were involved in espionage. Some of them were let into Canada because they were said to have valuable scientific knowledge, and the West wanted to make sure they didn't fall into communist hands.

Rodal notes that the British and the Americans took German atomic scientists and rocket researchers under a program known as Operation Paperclip, which saw such prominent figures as U-2 rocket designer Werner von Braun move to the U.S. to work on the American space program, which eventually put a man on the moon.

Rodal found that at least 71 German scientists also came to Canada, under a program called Operation Matchbox. They were mainly technicians and industrial researchers. Security screening was handled by the British and the Americans, who were more interested in beating the communists than in keeping ex-Nazis out of Canada.

These German scientists got jobs in private industry or were appointed to Canadian university posts. Some of them kept in close contact with their old colleagues in Britain and the U.S. They helped with the space program and other scientific activities.

The German scientists were admitted to Canada between 1947 and 1949, when government policy barred the immigration of all Germans. The rules were bent to let them into the country as "temporary workers" rather than immigrants. After the ban on Germans was lifted in 1950, they could apply for permanent residence, and eventually gain Canadian citizenship.

Rodal views these scientists as possible war criminals because their work was so important to the Nazi war effort. She says she suspected that several of them might have worked for I.G. Farben, a huge company whose directors were tried as war criminals in Germany after the war for using slave labor and other offences.

In still other cases, Rodal says, the government quietly helped suspected war criminals slip into Canada as a favor to the Vatican, which had close ties to the Germans during the war, and ended up helping a lot of fascists slip out of Europe after the fighting ended.

Deschênes recommended that Rodal's report be published by the government and widely distributed, but this was not done. Much of the report was eventually released in a photocopied form, however, after *The Toronto Star* and the Simon Wiesenthal Centre applied for it under the Access to Information Act.

The report says that two alleged Nazi war criminals were admitted to Canada in 1983, after documents relating to their pasts were destroyed. Rodal says the documents were destroyed by a German-born senior officer of the RCMP, along with other Mounties having sympathies which "inclined them towards leniency with regard to former Nazis."

Who were these two alleged Nazis who got into Canada this way? Their identities were revealed in Rodal's report, but taken out of the copy supplied to the Wiesenthal Centre. The explanation given for the deletion by the government was that it was "personal information."

The identities of the Mounties who helped them were also removed, on the grounds that disclosure "could reasonably be expected to be injurious to the enforcement of any law of Canada or a province or the conduct of lawful investigation."

A section of Rodal's report dealing with the attitudes of Prime Minister Pierre Trudeau was censored on the grounds that it was protected by "solicitor-client confidentiality" and "cabinet secrecy."

Eventually Trudeau himself admitted he had political reasons for not launching prosecutions. He said he was more interested in nation-building and appeasing ethnic minorities than in pursuing war criminals. Trudeau quietly vetoed legal action against war crimes suspect, even as his government publicly claimed to support such action, and even as Solicitor-General Robert Kaplan was trying to bring suspected war criminals to justice.

In one of the most interesting sections of her report, Rodal tells how the RCMP half-heartedly looked into allegations that Canada provided new homes from old Nazis who helped the Allies with Cold War espionage. The Mounties investigated the matter in 1983, after it was revealed that the American government had secretly helped Klaus Barbie settle in South American as a payoff for post-war intelligence services.

The RCMP found that Canadian visa intelligence officers relied heavily on checks by Allied intelligence agencies, so it would have been a simple matter for these agencies to help suspected war criminals get into Canada.

"The person could have applied to immigrate to Canada under his real or assumed name with the appropriate documentation being arranged by the intelligence agency," the RCMP concluded.

> When our Visa Control Officer subsequently requested a check through the intelligence agency, he would have been informed only that there was no adverse record concerning this person or no record of suspected/alleged war crimes at all. The prospective immigrant would then be passed by the security screening and subsequently issued a visa to immigrate to Canada.

But then the Mounties said that "there was no known effort on the part of Canadian officials to recruit or assist in the resettlement of persons known to be suspected war criminals," and that policies and directives in effect after the war were designed "to ensure that suspected war criminals would not be permitted to enter the country."

Rodal discovered that this was apparently an attempted white-wash, and that the Mounties later tried to correct themselves. She says a "top secret" report by Fred Yetter, the Mountie who tracked down Albert Rauca, concluded that the government did in fact knowingly take part in the resettlement of suspected war criminals.

Rodal quotes from Yetter's report, but just when the story starts to get good, the censors jump in. She quotes Yetter as saying that in 1954, Canadian officials discovered "the existence of an active and organized program run by the Research and Resettlement Branch of the U.S. Army."

The story is abruptly cut off at that point. There's a vague reference to "the role of Canadian authorities, in particular the RCMP and External Affairs," but again the details are squelched, this time with a reference to a secret hearing conducted by the Deschênes commission in May 1985.

Rodal goes on to talk about various police officers and government officials who expressed concern to the higher-ups about "irregularities" and "some forty persons" who had been presented for admission to Canada by the American Army, but again the details have been censored.

There's one anecdote, however, that sums things up nicely. It's about an applicant for admission to Canada who was turned down, and who was "presented by (censored) with a completely different set of documents and identity."

Rodal says that "officials at External Affairs expressed distaste for the whole affair, and Lester Pearson (then a senior civil servant and later Prime Minister) in particular felt that the Americans should take such people to the U.S., rather than unload them on others."

Days in Court

Imre Finta

CHAPTER 20

The Hungarian Charmer

Imre Finta, a dapper East European who loved the limelight, added new and unwanted notoriety to his life in 1987. At the age of 75, he became the first suspect to be charged under the new war crimes section of the Criminal Code.

Finta had been chosen by the Justice Department to be the test case for the made-in-Canada solution, but his background didn't suggest that he might someday wind up in court. In his native Hungary, back in the 1920s and 1930s, he had been a suave and colorful young fellow who won girls' hearts.

He dreamed of being an actor, but he ended up going to law school instead, and then on to a military academy. If he couldn't be a stage performer, then at least he could live the refined and leisurely life of a peacetime military officer.

But things didn't turn out that way. The Second World War came along, and that changed a lot of things for Finta, but if you jump ahead in time to the 1950s, you find him in Canada, where he became a bon vivant and a prosperous restaurant operator.

Finta promoted himself as the darling of the fashionable Toronto dining scene. He liked to have his picture taken with prominent people who came to his restaurants. He entertained, among others, French actor Maurice Chevalier, American singers Eartha Kitt and Joni James, and jazz great Louis Armstrong.

He was the sort of man who kissed women's hands, and he loved to pose for photographs with celebrities who patronized his restaurant. He was the same old Finta, the same theatrical type who had dreamed of being on stage. He was a "showboat," both before and after the war. He was also a gentleman, and he certainly never gave any indication that he was a Jew-hater, either before or after the war.

But during the war, he got caught up in the events of his times. The evilness of the Nazi era engulfed him. If the times had been different, he might have left the military to become an actor, or remained in the service and become an honorable Hungarian officer.

Instead, he became a Nazi collaborator. In 1944, he was involved in the forced deportation of more than 8,600 Hungarian Jews. Some of these unfortunate people were sent to Austria to work as slave laborers. The rest were shipped off to concentration camps in Poland, where most of them were killed.

The exact role played by Finta in these activities, and the reasons why he did what he did, were the key issues when he went on trial in Canada in 1989, 45 years after the events in question.

Was he a willing participant and an agent of the Holocaust? Was he, as the Crown alleged, responsible for the confinement of these Jews and their subsequent deportation? Did he have any freedom of action, or was he under the thumb of the SS? Was he just following orders? Did he believe those orders were lawful? Those were the questions the Canadian jury was asked to consider.

It wasn't an easy task, because the events were remote from those jurors, in both time and distance. The scene of Finta's alleged crimes was a small city in southern Hungary called Szeged. The date was June 1944. It was quite a stretch, both chronologically and geographically, from the late 1980s in Toronto, where Finta's trial was held. This made it difficult for the prosecutors to build a successful case against Finta.

All 12 of the men and women on the jury were too young to have any recollection of the war, and few of them had even heard of Szeged, a city near the Romanian border about 150 kilometres south of Budapest.

When the eight women and four men on the jury initially looked at Finta, they didn't see the one-time monster that the prosecution tried to make him out to be. Rather, they saw a dapper, white-haired gentleman with a courtly manner and a pleasant smile, who walked with a limp and carried a cane. It was hard to imagine this old man as he was said to have been in 1944 – a 32-year-old police officer, dressed in a snappy green uniform, strutting around in shiny boots.

It was tough to see the old fellow as having once been a big shot in the small town where he grew up, lording it over the Jews he had once been friendly with, before the Nazis came. But the people in the Justice Department's newly formed war crimes unit thought they had a good case against Finta.

They were sure that they could persuade the jury to see Finta as he once was, and that the much-belated prosecution of this old man was a good start to what they hoped would be a series of successful war crimes trials under the new, made-in-Canada law.

They had chosen Finta to be a test case because they had a great deal of evidence against him, and because they had been under a lot of pressure from Jewish activists to make an example of him. His celebrity as a restaurant operator, and the way in which he deliberately drew attention to himself, made it seem to the Jews as if he was flaunting his war crimes.

The Jews were keen to see him prosecuted, even though he didn't have "bloody hands." This was the term used to describe someone who he had actually killed Jews. Finta had never been accused of pulling the trigger himself. Simply, he had played a part in the process which resulted in the deaths, but that was enough for the Canadian Jewish activists.

They saw the Holocaust as a crime which involved not only the actual killers, but the people who had organized and administered things. The massive killing operation, they realized, could not have been carried out without a lot of "support staff." Without people like Finta, they maintained, there could have been no Holocaust.

Rumors about Finta had been circulating among Canadian Jews since the 1950s, soon after his arrival in Canada, in part because he drew so much attention to himself. In 1953, he opened a dining spot in Toronto called the Candlelight Cafe. He advertised his business heavily, and turned the spotlight on himself as the celebrity owner.

Four years later, he renovated the place and created an even fancier spot which he called the Moulin Rouge, to suggest a connection with Paris, where he had lived for a time after the war.

He promoted his businesses and himself vigorously, and produced a fancy brochure in which he told an edited version of his life story. He described his early years in Hungary, and said he had danced on the stage and yearned to be an actor.

The brochure went on to say that he went to a military academy, but didn't mention anything about his activities in Szeged. It jumped ahead to late 1944, when the Nazis were chased out of Hungary by the Russians. Finta said he fled to Germany, where he was arrested and spent a year as an American prisoner of war. Then he worked in a variety of European hotels and restaurants, learning the arts of cooking and hospitality, before coming to Canada in 1951 and working his way up from humble beginnings as a cook to become a restaurant owner.

Finta sold his interest in the Moulin Rouge in 1971, but Toronto Jews continued to keep track of him. In 1974, Nazi hunter Simon Wiesenthal wrote to Canada's ambassador in Vienna complaining about Finta's alleged war crimes. This sparked a story in *The Toronto Star* which quoted Finta as saying he had saved at least 10 Jewish families from the Nazis, but that other Jews hated him because he was unable to help them, too.

In the early 1980s, a Holocaust survivor named Sabina Citron, who had escaped death in a Polish concentration camp, and who was a leader of the Canadian Holocaust Remembrance Association, publicly accused Finta of being a war criminal.

She had become active in the Jewish community after a group of neo-Nazis demonstrated in downtown Toronto. Citron believed that if something was not done to fight back, Naziism might make a comeback. Citron vowed that if there was anything she could do about it, this wouldn't happen.

Finta responded to Citron's allegations by publicly calling her a liar. Citron, recognizing a good opportunity when she saw it, sued Finta for libel. The case dragged through the courts for five years.

Finta finally ended up having to pay Citron $30,000 plus legal costs. The *Toronto Sun* newspaper, which had carried Finta's claim that Citron was a liar, quietly settled a libel action brought by Citron for an undisclosed amount. In another civil case, Finta sued CTV after the television network's W5 show linked him to war crimes. At the time Finta was charged, that libel action was still before the courts.

Eventually, Finta dropped the suit, but he was ordered to pay $177,000 in legal costs. His house was seized by a court order to pay those costs.

In the meantime, the government, urged on by Citron, decided to prosecute Finta. That's when the case moved into the criminal court system, where his guilt or innocence would finally be decided by the jury which started hearing the case in late 1989, about two years after Finta was charged.

Finta was one of the hundreds of alleged war criminals who were investigated by the Deschênes commission in 1985 and 1986. (Deschênes had come up with a list of 20 prime suspects, and had recommended that immediate action be taken to prosecute them. See Chapter 17.) While that list was kept secret, Finta's name could well have been on it, since the government moved so quickly against him, and since it chose him as its test case under the new legislation which had been enacted upon Deschênes' recommendations.

Finta himself wasn't surprised when he was picked up by the RCMP in late 1987. He had been planning to take a holiday in Florida, and had told the Mounties about his plans in advance. He was aware they were investigating him, and didn't want to give them the impression that he was trying to sneak out of the country.

But when he was taken into custody by the Mounties on December 9, 1987 in Hamilton, Ontario, while waiting for a bus to nearby Buffalo, N.Y., that's the impression that was created in the public mind. It looked as if the Mounties had caught him running away.

After his arrest at the bus station, Finta was taken to the Don Jail in Toronto, where he remained for a few days, until relatives came up with the $100,000 he needed to make bail. The government charged him with robbery and with the kidnapping and confining more than 8,600 Jews who had been rounded up by the Nazis and their cohorts in Szeged in 1944.

They also charged him with the manslaughter of an unspecified number of Jews who died after being loaded on trains for transportation to a work camp in Austria and an extermination camp in Poland.

The arrest made headlines across Canada, and much was made of the fact that Finta was headed for the States. Later, when the details of the arrest came out, Finta's lawyer suggested that it was stage-managed to make Finta look like he was fleeing, but if that really was what they intended, the Mounties never publicly admitted it.

They did, however, eventually have to explain to a judge how they started out to arrest Finta with almost military efficiency, and ended up bungling the case so badly that they were unable to bring before the jury an important piece of evidence against Finta.

The head of the three-man squad which picked up Finta was RCMP Sgt. Fred Yetter, who had tracked down Albert Rauca, the former German SS officer found living in Canada and extradited to West Germany. Yetter and two other Mounties followed Finta around Hamilton for hours before they arrested him at the bus terminal, but when they took him to an RCMP office to question him, they didn't provide Finta with a Hungarian interpreter.

Although many people said he spoke good English, Finta was able to convince a judge that his English wasn't good enough to enable him to understand the routine warning that the police were required to give him before questioning him. Under the law, they had to ensure that he understood that anything he said could be used against him later, in court.

When the Mounties questioned Finta after his arrest, he made a key admission. They showed him a train schedule which was used for the deportation of Szeged's Jews in 1944. Finta confirmed to the Mounties that it was his signature which appeared on the schedule, making it appear as if he had ordered the schedule, or at least approved of it.

But the judge at Finta's trial refused to allow that incriminating admission to the RCMP to be used as evidence, so the jury was never told about it. A key ingredient in the Crown's case was thus lost.

The jury was also not informed about a second incriminating point against Finta. It turned out that after he fled from Hungary, he had been tried in his absence. In 1948, a communist tribunal sentenced him to five years in jail for committing war crimes. That information was deemed by the judge to be prejudicial to Finta's right to a fair trial in Canada, but in a way it might almost have been to Finta's advantage if it had been made known to the jurors.

If all the communists did was sentence him to five years (and later even that jail term was commuted), it suggested that what Finta had done couldn't have been all that bad. Many other people sentenced by communist courts for war crimes received the death penalty or life imprisonment. It's impossible to say whether the Hungarian conviction and the admission to the RCMP about his signature would have made any difference to the eventual outcome of the case.

The trial began on November 22, 1989, almost two years after Finta's arrest. Much of the time between the arrest and trial had been taken up with legal motions and arguments. Associate Chief Justice Frank Callaghan of the Ontario Supreme Court had ruled in the Crown's favor in a pre-trial hearing on whether or not the new Canadian war crimes law was constitutional.

This was an important victory for the prosecution, which also took advantage of the delay in the start of the trial to send teams to Hungary and Israel to gather more evidence against Finta.

Mr. Justice Archie Campbell of the Ontario Supreme Court presided at the trial. Campbell and the 12 jurors soon learned that Finta was born in 1912 in Kolozvar, which at the time was in Romania, but later became part of Hungary. As a young man, he had wanted to be an actor, and in 1935 he was photographed in heavy makeup with a rag doll after his performance as a ventriloquist. But he ended up studying law.

Later, he attended a military academy, and in 1939 he was commissioned as a second lieutenant in a para-military outfit called the Royal Hungarian Gendarmerie, which provided police services in rural areas.

During most of the war years, Hungary was governed by fascists, and several anti-semitic laws were passed. Hungary was a German ally, but it resisted rounding up Jews the way the Nazis did. Eventually, the right-wing government led by Miklos Horthy was turfed out by the Germans, who were keen to see the Jews of Hungary exterminated, and also feared that the Hungarians would sell them out and side with the advancing Soviets. They replaced the Horthy government with a puppet regime.

By March 1944, Finta had reached the rank of captain and had been appointed as commander of the detective division of the gendarmerie in his old home town of Szeged. That same month, German troops invaded Hungary. The Nazis established a command structure which was headed by SS chief Heinrich Himmler, and ran down through various officials in Budapest to police and SS units operating throughout Hungary.

The new government quickly developed a plan for the purging of the Jews from Hungary, and circulated a decree which was known as the Baky Order. It was addressed to the nation's various military and police officials, including officers of the gendarmerie's detective subdivision, and that included Finta. Thus, he was able to argue in court later that he was acting under written orders which had been issued by the lawful government of Hungary, and ultimately the Supreme Court of Canada accepted this as a valid defence.

Dated April 7, 1944, the Baky Order said that the "final solution" to the Jewish problem in Hungary would be carried out in phases. First, the Jews would be isolated. Then their property would be expropriated and they would be put into ghettos in their home communities. Next, they would be brought to larger centres, where they would be put into temporary concentration camps until they could be loaded aboard trains and shipped out of the country.

Hungary was divided into six zones, each under the command of the gendarmerie. The city of Szeged was designated as a concentration centre in Zone 4. Jews from Szeged and surrounding communities were rounded up and confined in a fenced-in brickyard. By June 20, 1944, an estimated 8,617 Jews were in the brickyard, which consisted of a large open area containing a big kiln, a chimney and several buildings used for drying bricks. The Jews were packed together in this filthy place. They slept on the ground.

Repeated announcements were made over a loudspeaker ordering the Jews to surrender their remaining gold, jewelry and other valuables, on pain of death. In the last week of June, the Jews were marched from the brickyard to the train station, where they were forced to climb into boxcars. Two trains took many of the Jews to a labor camp in Strasshof, Austria. A third train took the rest to the extermination camp in Auschwitz, Poland.

From 70 to 90 Jews were crammed into each boxcar, which measured about eight metres by two metres. They were so crowded that many people were forced to remain standing. The doors were padlocked, and the only openings for air were small windows in the upper corners of each car. Usually the cars contained two buckets. One was for water and the other was used as a toilet, but conditions were so crowded that most of the prisoners were forced to relieve themselves where they stood or sat. Some of the Jews, mostly old people, died during the trip, but normally the guards didn't permit bodies to be removed before the train reached its destination, and so the overcrowded cars stank of both human excrement and death.

The Crown built its case against Finta doggedly and methodically. Dozens of witnesses were interviewed, many of them in Hungary and Israel, where their evidence was taken with the help of translators and recorded on videotape. The prosecution didn't have many star witnesses.

Only two of the 43 people who testified against Finta were able to identify him as the captain who had been in charge at the brickyard, since they had known him when he was young and recognized him in his new incarnation. The defence suggested that these two women might have been lying and accused them of trying to outdo each other in fabricating stories about Finta.

Mostly, the Crown tried to build its case against Finta bit by bit, but when it was presented to the jury in a piecemeal fashion over the course of six long months, the trial seemed to drag on and on, and there was plenty of potential for distraction and confusion. For example, a concentration camp survivor named Meir Schweiger told the jury that a Hungarian officer who identified himself as Imre Finta supervised the loading of a train that took Jews to a camp at Birkenau.

But Schweiger was not asked to identify the man in court, or to say if he was the same Imre Finta whom he had seen in Szeged. It was only later that pictures of Finta were presented as evidence, and an attempt was made to link the photos with the man Schweiger talked about.

There was also a lot of evidence about what happened to the Jews of Szeged in general. While much of it was disgusting and horrifying, the cumulative effect was to produce a sense of numbness in the jurors, especially since the Crown didn't directly link a lot of it to Finta.

But sometimes the evidence was riveting, as was the case when one of those who identified Finta – a 73-year-old woman named Margit Hahn – claimed she had been Finta's teenage girlfriend in the 1930s. She said she lost track of him until the day in 1944 when he came across a gendarme helping her and her mother load their baggage onto a train bound for Auschwitz. Hahn said Finta cursed her. "He called me a stinking whore, a Jewish whore, all kinds of dirt," Hahn testified.

She said that he was so angry that he "roared like a wild beast," and she described the way in which Finta was "beating his boots with a stick." She recalled the old days, when she and Finta dated for several months, and how he had been a pleasant young man whom she called Gosling because "his hair was a shade of green and yellow like the feathers of a freshly hatched gosling."

Another witness was Edith Lakos, a Jew who lived across the street from Finta in Szeged and knew him when she was a teenager in the 1930s. "He was a nice, blonde good-looking young man," Lakos recalled. She didn't see him again until June 1944, when she and her parents were in the Szeged brickyard.

The last witnesses testified in April 1990, and the trial was adjourned until early May. Then it was time for the lawyers to make their closing arguments and the judge to charge the jury.

CHAPTER 21

"I Love Jewish People"

Prosecutor Christopher Amerasinghe had spent five months calling witnesses to prove that Imre Finta was a war criminal. In May 1990, he spent three more days summing up his convoluted case.

Amerasinghe reviewed the testimony of the 43 prosecution witnesses, but in an interesting twist he became a defence attorney of sorts himself. His "client" was the new war crimes law under which Finta had been charged.

Amerasinghe defended the law, which had been attacked by some people as unjust and unfair. He argued that prosecuting old war criminals was not a waste of time and the taxpayers' money.

The prosecutor said crimes against humanity were a violation of international law, not just Canadian law. He said that if a person committed such crimes in a foreign country and subsequently came to live in Canada, then Canada had a duty to bring that person to justice.

He argued that the anti-semitic laws in Hungary in 1944 were "so manifestly wrong in substance" that they were illegal. He said Finta should have realized that and refused to obey those laws. Amerasinghe said the former police captain wasn't an underling who could claim he was forced to obey orders. Instead, said the prosecutor, Finta was in a position of authority, and therefore able to play a leading role in the anti-Jewish atrocities which occurred.

The prosecutor denied that politics motivated the laying of the charges against Finta. He said the accused man was being treated no differently than any other person who was guilty of serious crimes in Canada. "It's not a political charge," Amerasinghe insisted. "It's not unfair."

But Finta's lawyer, Douglas Christie, saw things differently. Christie maintained that it was unfair to blame Finta for what went on in Szeged, because he wasn't the man in charge. It was the Nazis who were calling the shots, Christie said. Anything that Finta did, his lawyer maintained, was done under Nazi orders.

Earlier, during his cross-examination of prosecution witnesses, Christie had compared the events in Szeged with events which had happened in Canada during the war. Christie pointed to the similarity between the deportation of the Jews from Hungary and the way in which people of Japanese origin had been uprooted from their homes in western Canada and taken by the RCMP to isolated areas. The Canadian government ordered these forced removals as a security measure soon after the Japanese bombed Pearl Harbor, fearing that the Japanese-Canadians might assist the enemy in a possible invasion or sabotage on Canada's west coast.

Christie asked rhetorically whether the RCMP officers who carried out those orders should have refused to obey them, since the Canadian government later admitted that these orders had been illegal. The government decided, in hindsight, that the forced removals had deprived the Japanese-Canadians of their civil rights. Ultimately, the government issued a formal apology, but no one was ever punished for the wrongs that had been done to the Japanese-Canadians.

Amerasinghe rejected the comparison, arguing that the Canadian government might have been wrong, but it only amounted to discrimination, and it was not done brutally. He said what was done to the Jews fell into the much more serious category of persecution, and resulted in massive suffering and death. Judge Campbell later told the jurors to ignore the question of whether or not the Mounties should have disobeyed their orders. "You and I have enough to do in this case," Campbell told the jurors, "without trying someone else for alleged offences."

Christie was well known to most Canadians for his representation of Ernst Zundel and James Keegstra. They had been defendants in highly publicized trials which revolved around the issue of anti-semitism, and some Jewish activists had criticized Christie's legal tactics in those cases. In the Finta case, Christie went after Jewish activists indirectly, without naming anyone.

"Some people," he alleged, "never want to see the fighting end, the dredging up of old grievances, opening up old wounds." He suggested that such people were blaming Finta for all their old suffering, and that they were motivated by a desire to gain revenge, not to see justice done.

Christie sought to make the war crimes law the real defendant in the case, calling it the "most diabolically twisted, convoluted piece of legislation I have ever had to deal with." He said that because the law contained no time limit, people like Finta could be hauled into court decades after their alleged offences, when it was virtually impossible to find reliable witnesses to testify either for or against them. If Canada was so keen on trying war criminals, Christie said, it should have brought them to trial when the evidence was fresh and a suspect had a fair chance to defend himself.

Christie said his decision not to call Finta or any other defence witnesses to the stand was not evidence of guilt. He pointed out that the onus was on the Crown to prove its charges, not on Finta to disprove them. He painted the government as a fat cat with unlimited resources to go chasing around the world to collect evidence, while Finta didn't have the money to do that.

He argued that the prosecution witnesses were unreliable, and that they contradicted each other frequently and were ganging up on Finta. Christie recalled one incident in which a man in the audience was caught making hand signs to a witness who was giving evidence. Christie called this "teamwork testimony," and claimed that other witnesses had passed on information to each other before they took the stand. He called this "testimony by gossip."

Christie admitted that Finta was a captain of the gendarmes in Szeged, and that the Jews were loaded on the trains. At one point, he suggested that Finta might have been present in the brickyard holding area when some of the Jews' jewelry was confiscated. But the defence lawyer stressed that Finta was not in charge. The Nazis were. Finta was just following orders, and because it was wartime, he could have been shot if he didn't do what the Germans told him to do.

He said Finta wasn't responsible for widespread anti-semitism in Hungary, and that he might have believed the Jews were being deported because they posed a threat to the security of the country. The Soviet army was advancing on Hungary, and the Jews might have tried to help them, Christie said. Therefore, Finta might have believed the deportation of the Jews was not a war crime, but rather an evacuation required for military reasons.

When Christie had finished his summation, Judge Campbell adjourned the trial for 12 days, and then he addressed the jury himself. His role was to explain the complexities of the law to the jurors, and put the arguments of the Crown and the defence into perspective.

Campbell contradicted some of the things Christie had said. He was especially harsh on the defence attorney's remarks about the "diabolical" nature of the war crimes law. Campbell said the law was constitutional, and it conformed to the principles of fundamental justice. He warned the jurors against acquitting Finta in a misguided effort to "send a message" to the authorities that they disagreed with the law, or that they felt it was too late to be trying war criminals.

The judge also responded to a suggestion that Christie had made that the jurors themselves could be in legal peril. Christie had said that the jurors might conceivably find themselves brought before another court, 45 years in the future, to answer for their actions in this court. He said that the prosecution of Finta might in the future be deemed to have been wrong. He asked the jurors who they would call on to defend them, if they should ever end up as defendants themselves, for being part of the Finta trial.

Campbell assured the jurors that their job could not be considered persecution of Finta. He said it was misleading to compare their function to the actions of someone who might have been carrying out orders in a military hierarchy and who was subsequently charged with war crimes.

But the judge also responded to points which Amerasinghe had raised. The judge said it would be wrong for the jurors to think that if they should decide to acquit Finta, they would somehow be denying that the Holocaust ever took place. Similarly, he said, an acquittal of Finta would not be an affront to the Jews who had suffered.

He told the jurors to be careful about photos which had been used by the prosecution in an attempt to identify Finta. The pictures were taken 21 years apart. The judge described the eye-witness identification of Finta by some of the Crown's witnesses as "very weak." He said that of the five witnesses who placed Finta at the railway station where the Jews were loaded, only two had known Finta from before the war.

Earlier, Christie had contended that these two witnesses, Margit Hahn and Eva Liptak, should not be believed. He said they had competed to see which of them could be "the most mean and vicious" toward Finta, and he had characterized Hahn as "a bitter and vindictive liar."

The case went to the jury on the afternoon of Thursday, May 24, 1990. While the jury was out, Campbell heard objections from both lawyers to his closing remarks to the jury. Both Amerasinghe and Christie maintained that in one way or another, the judge had not been fair enough or clear enough in his instructions to the jury. The judge recalled the jurors to clarify a few points.

Then he told them to continue their deliberations, but not to make a final decision until he recalled them once more and told them there would be no further instructions. It was a confusing ending to a long and complicated case, and observers wondered what the jurors were making of it all.

Some people expected the jury would take a long time to reach a verdict, because of the importance and complexity of the case. But they were wrong. The jurors made up their minds quickly. The next afternoon, after having spent only about 12 hours in deliberation, and just 20 minutes after Campbell told them there would be no further instructions from the bench and they should go ahead and decide the case, they came back into court with their verdict.

They acquitted Finta on all counts.

Why they found Finta not guilty was the subject of much discussion, speculation and educated guessing, in the hours and days after the trial. The jurors themselves couldn't be asked about it, and what went on in the jury room must forever remain a secret. American journalists can interview jurors to learn what went on behind closed doors, to find out which jurors initially voted which way, and so forth. It's a standard conclusion to a big trial in the U.S., and it helps people understand why things came out the way they did. But this can't be done in Canada.

Under Canadian law, what goes on in the jury room is deemed to be confidential, even after the trial has ended. Jurors can be punished for speaking out about their deliberations, and journalists can get into trouble for approaching jurors after a trial is over. The theory is that this will help make sure that jurors focus on their prime responsibility, which is to come up with a unanimous and just verdict.

If they don't have to worry about explaining themselves later to lawyers, inquisitive reporters and others, they can give their full attention to the task.

So what the jurors thought remained secret, but there was nothing to stop Finta himself from offering his reactions on the case and the verdict. He had remained silent throughout the trial, and seemed glad to talk to reporters when it was over. "The jury found me not guilty," Finta said. "That's Canada. This verdict was Canada."

He complained that other people had made money off the war crimes issue, while he was at the heart of it and had lost everything that he had. He said a movie called "The Holocaust" had made a $6-million profit, and another movie called *The Music Box*, which coincidentally was about an accused Hungarian war criminal, had made $12-million. Finta noted that his house had been seized to pay the costs of CTV in the libel action he had launched against the network.

"Now," Finta said, "I would like to make some money." He announced that a Hungarian publisher would produce his autobiography, and that he hoped it would be translated into English and German. He said "My Life, My Love, My Fate" was going to be the book's title.

He told reporters that he was "100 per cent innocent," and that he was never a Nazi collaborator. "I'm a Bohemian," he said, "a show business man, not a murderer." He also stressed that he was not anti-semitic. "I love Jewish people," Finta said.

But a lot of Jewish people didn't love Imre Finta. They were stunned and embittered by the verdict. Helen Smolack, chairman of the Canadian Holocaust Remembrance Association, said that "it makes us lose faith in the justice system in Canada." Holocaust survivor Eugene Lawrence called the jurors "naive," and said that "people cannot comprehend really what happened." Spokesmen for various Jewish groups had similar sentiments.

But *Maclean's* magazine columnist Barbara Amiel saw things differently. She criticized the negative Jewish response to the verdict.

"Speaking as a Jew," Amiel said,

I can't help feeling a profound sense of shame at such comments. Are these Jewish leaders not content yet? Virtually single-handedly, they have created the awful situation we now face because the trial took place: Jews feel the acquittal is a personal slap in the face, while, at the same time, Canada's teeny group of neo-Nazis are having a celebration.

Amiel questioned the fairness of prosecuting lower-ranking former soldiers and policemen for war crimes which happened a long time ago in another place. She argued that imposing contemporary standards and values was unfair.

"The point," she concluded,

is that you cannot demand that individuals be much better than the social milieu in which they live. Most people do accept the shibboleths of their times, just as Finta did.

Once upon a time, we understood that fundamental truth about the human condition. We understood that distances of geography and time produce different moral climates which make it distinctly unwise – and unfair – to judge from the outside.

Arnold Fradkin, deputy director of the Justice Department's war crimes unit, said the acquittal of Finta wouldn't slow the pace of investigations of other suspected war criminals. "It's full steam ahead," he said. At that time, the war crimes unit was looking into about 45 other cases.

Two more suspects, Michael Pawlowski and Stephen Reistetter, had been charged under the new war crimes law, while the government was using another technique against a third man, Jacob Luitjens. The authorities were trying to strip him of his citizenship and deport him.

Meanwhile, the jury's acquittal of Finta didn't mean the government was giving up on his case. The war crimes unit filed an appeal, hoping to win a new trial and a chance to bring Finta before another jury. The Ontario Court of Appeal turned down that appeal in 1992, but the prosecutors still didn't quit. They took the Finta case to the Supreme Court of Canada.

The nation's top court upheld the constitutional validity of the war crimes law. But the court also said that the defence of "just following orders" could be successfully used by a defendant to win an acquittal if he believed those orders were lawful. The court concluded that "there was such an air of compulsion and threat to the accused that the accused had no alternative but to obey the order."

In effect, the nation's highest court validated the just-following-orders defence. So the government's legal action against Finta finally came to an end in March 1994. The ruling seemingly made it impossible for the Crown to convict anyone under the war crimes law, and eventually Justice Minister Allan Rock admitted that the ruling made future prosecutions unlikely.

The Supreme Court ruling was the kiss of death to the high-minded scheme proposed by Jules Deschênes and adopted by the government to try war criminals in Canada.

The made-in-Canada solution was a flop.

CHAPTER 22

Shot Down Like Animals

There's a small grave marker in Eastern Europe which reads: "Here lie in peace the remains of people shot like animals."

Michael Pawlowski, who was arrested by the RCMP in December 1989, was allegedly one of the cold-blooded killers who shot these people, but when the case went to court, a much different version of the truth came out, and Pawlowski wasn't convicted of anything.

The prosecutors said that in 1942, Pawlowski and others killed some 80 Poles near a village, as well as 10 more Jews in or near a cemetery.

But the really big crime involved some 400 Jewish victims, who were taken to a remote site off a major highway, forced to climb into a pit, and killed in a single day. This is the place which has the grave marker.

Nine years after the slaughter, Big Mike, as Pawlowski was often called because of his husky build, came to Canada. He started working in a lumber mill in Renfrew, Ontario, a small Ottawa Valley town. He soon got a better job as a carpenter with Ontario Hydro, and worked there for 30 years before he retired. After that, he spent much of his time puttering around in his garden.

Before his arrest, Pawlowski was generally regarded as a nice guy by the people of Renfrew, where he had lived for 38 years. He sold fruits and vegetables at the Saturday morning market, and won prizes for his roses from the local horticultural society. He was friendly with his neighbors and nice to their kids, but he pretty much minded his own business. He didn't fit the stereotype of the old Nazi war criminal who was still a monster, despite the passage of time.

Pawlowski used his own name, didn't try to disguise his appearance, and made no attempt to conceal the fact that he had come from a part of Eastern Europe where some of the worst atrocities of the war had taken place. But he flatly denied that he had taken any part in them, and right from the start, he said the communists were lying and fabricating evidence against him. As subsequent events were to show, he may well have been right about that.

Pawlowski's arrest came as a surprise to almost everyone. He had previously been unknown to Canadian Jewish groups, despite the fact that they had assembled lists containing the names of hundreds of suspected war criminals. It turned out that the Soviets had quietly fingered Pawlowski, about four years before he was arrested. They had sent his name, along with affidavits from witnesses, to the Justice Department in 1985, when Jules Deschênes was appealing to people with information about war criminals in Canada to come forward.

The Soviets were happy to oblige, but the lack of publicity in this case didn't fit in with their typical pattern of trying to use such accusations to embarrass the Canadian government for being soft on war criminals. In the past, when the Soviets had claimed that other Canadian immigrants were war criminals, they had sent out news releases. This time they were discreet.

Deschênes looked into the Soviet allegations about Pawlowski, then turned his findings over to the Justice Department, which established a special unit in 1987 to prosecute war criminals. Officials in Ottawa soon worked out a deal with the Soviets to permit Canadian investigators to go to the U.S.S.R. to gather evidence, and one of the first cases they pursued was Pawlowski's.

RCMP officers, government lawyers and historians went to the Soviet Union to examine documents and interview witnesses. They were impressed, and thought there was strong evidence against Pawlowski. The top people in the war crimes unit became convinced they could build a solid case in a Canadian courtroom, but the final decision was up to the man in charge of the Justice Department. The war crimes law under which Pawlowski would be charged stipulated that charges could only be laid with the consent of the Attorney General of Canada.

Doug Lewis held that position in the Progressive-Conservative government of Brian Mulroney. It was Mulroney's government which had established the Deschênes commission, amended the law to permit the prosecution of suspects in Canadian courts, and set up the war crimes unit. The Mulroney Tories had gone where the Liberals had feared to tread. They saw the Pawlowski case as a good chance to make good on their commitment to take action against war criminals.

The arrest make front-page headlines and was the lead item in newscasts across Canada. Jewish spokesmen were brimming with praise for the government. The Pawlowski case looked like the perfect opportunity for the government to demonstrate the effectiveness of its made-in-Canada solution to the problem of dealing with war criminals in Canada. Trying suspects in Canada was seen as an innovative way to get around the problem of sending them back to the Soviet Union for trial.

But what wasn't fully appreciated until the Pawlowski case was that such a trial in Canada still needed evidence and witnesses from behind the Iron Curtain. This created a lot of difficulties. Witnesses might be available in the U.S.S.R., but how was their testimony going to be presented to a jury in Canada? How reliable was that testimony going to be if it was procured by the Soviets through coercive interrogation methods? Soviet-supplied documents might be made available to the Canadians, but what if the Soviets withheld some of the relevant ones which might help the defendant?

Jewish groups, eager to see war criminals punished, downplayed such fears. They said those who raised them were just playing into the war criminals' hands. Some even went so far as to ridicule people who were leery of evidence from behind the Iron Curtain, suggesting that they were racists or knee-jerk anti-communists who didn't care about the truth.

They claimed that Soviet evidence had been found to be valid by war crimes prosecutors in the U.S. and other countries, and that there had never been a case in which the Soviets had been found to be lying. They said the Soviets didn't have to lie. So many war criminals had done so many evil things in Eastern Europe that all the Soviets had to do was tell the truth.

But fears that Soviet evidence was unreliable turned out to be valid in the Pawlowski case. There was good reason to believe that a lot of the evidence had been trumped up, while other relevant material, which tended to show that Pawlowski was innocent, had been deliberately suppressed.

This wasn't immediately apparent, however, and it never really came to the attention of the Canadian public, because Pawlowski didn't go to trial. If he had, the serious defects in the Soviet evidence would have been revealed. The public was left with the mistaken impression that the judge had been unreasonable in refusing to allow the Soviet evidence to be used.

The charges against Pawlowski dated back to 1942, when the Holocaust was at its peak. Pawlowski was said to have been a member of a police death squad which killed 490 people, most of them Jews. The scene of the alleged crimes was an area of Eastern Europe which, in 1989, was known as the Byelorussian Republic of the U.S.S.R. Today it's an independent nation known as Belarus.

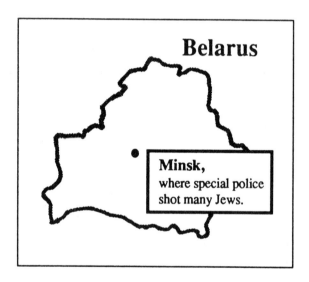

The murders were said to have occurred near the villages of Snov and Yeskovichi in the Minsk region. Before the war, the area had been part of Poland. It was taken over by the Soviets in 1939, after Hitler and Stalin made a deal to carve Poland up between them. In 1941, after Hitler turned on his former ally and launched a massive attack to the east, the Soviets were chased out, and the Germans marched in. Three years later, the Soviets took it back again as they pushed the Germans back on the Eastern Front.

The Canadian prosecutors alleged that Pawlowski was one of the local men who threw in their lot with the Nazis. The prosecutors said that after the Germans were beaten, Pawlowski somehow managed to escape, and thereby elude Soviet justice. The Soviets punished many other people from the area for collaborating with the Nazis, and it was these alleged accomplices who provided the most damaging evidence against Pawlowski. His former colleagues claimed that he was right in there with them, wiping out Jewish men, women and children.

But Pawlowski painted a much different picture. As he told it, he was an ordinary young fellow who struggled to survive the chaotic events which swirled around him during the war. He said that after the Germans arrived in 1941, they threatened to shoot his parents if he didn't join the Nazi-like police unit. He said he was appointed second in command of the detachment not because he was pro-Nazi, but because he could read and write. Those were skills he had acquired while he was studying for the priesthood before the war, he said.

He acknowledged that a lot of Jews and other civilians had been killed, but he denied any personal involvement. Pawlowski said he was not the sort of person to have committed even one murder, let alone hundreds. He said he was a good Roman Catholic and he never helped the Nazis kill the Jews.

His brother, Alex Pawlowski, backed him up. He said that Michael was "quite religious. He wouldn't hurt a fly that was sitting on his nose." Some of the people in Renfrew also supported him. A neighbor described Pawlowski as "one of the nicest, most honest gentlemen I ever knew." Others said he was the grandfatherly type, and that he was always nice to the neighborhood children.

There were eight charges against him. Four of them alleged that he had committed war crimes, and four parallel counts, dealing with the same events, alleged that he had committed crimes against humanity. The overlapping charges were laid because this was a relatively new area of law, and there was some question as to what constituted a war crime, and what constituted a crime against humanity. The new law dealt with both concepts, and the prosecution played it safe by double-charging Pawlowski on each count.

Pawlowski was arrested on a Monday afternoon. He spent the night in an Ottawa jail. The next day, he appeared before Mr. Justice James Chadwick of the Ontario Supreme Court. He walked haltingly and stooped slightly as he was escorted by police into a small courtroom. He watched the proceedings through half-closed eyes, which he at times wiped with a tissue.

One of his lawyers, Donald Bayne, told reporters later that Pawlowski had known for several months that he was being investigated, and had offered to co-operate with the authorities, but the RCMP had arrested him at home instead of calling him down to the police station with his lawyer. Bayne called the arrest a "media production" and suggested the government was trying to milk the case for maximum publicity.

Pawlowski was released on bail, but the judge ordered him and his wife Mary to put up their home as collateral, and imposed other conditions to make sure Pawlowski wouldn't skip the country. Judge Chadwick ordered him to appear in court again about a month later.

That's when the Crown's case started to fall apart.

Instead of bringing Pawlowski to trial quickly, the prosecutors asked the judge for permission to send what was known as a "commission" to the Soviet Union to take evidence. This was because the Soviet witnesses refused to come to Canada to testify. They said they were too old and didn't want to undergo the stress of having to appear in court in a foreign country. They were also concerned about having to leave their families, and about not being able to speak English.

The commission was to be made up of a group of Canadians, including a judge, prosecution and defence lawyers and translators, who would all go to the Soviet Union. Witnesses would appear before the commission in a Soviet courtroom, which would be presided over jointly by the Canadian judge and a Soviet judge. They would be questioned by the lawyers, and their testimony would be translated and videotaped. These tapes would be shown to the judge and jury at Pawlowski's trial in Canada.

It was trial by TV.

This procedure had been employed for some of the evidence in the Finta case, but most of the witnesses in that case had come to Canada to give their evidence in person. In the Pawlowski case, the Crown wanted virtually all the evidence to be on videotape. The judge didn't like the sounds of that. He felt it would be unfair to Pawlowski. Jewish activists accused him of being overly concerned about the rights of an accused war criminal, but one of the main arguments for the made-in-Canada solution had been that the rights of defendant would be protected.

The judge said Pawlowski would be unable to confront his accusers, face to face, and the jurors would be unable to take the measure of the witnesses and assess their credibility in person. "The jury in this case would be in a very difficult, if not impossible, position in attempting to assess credibility solely on the videotaped evidence of these Crown witnesses," Chadwick said.

The judge also noted that the affidavits supplied by the Soviets indicated that nine of the 12 witnesses had been convicted in the U.S.S.R. as traitors or Nazi collaborators. He felt that their statements were suspicious. He said they seemed to be confessions which had been obtained by Soviet police during long and intimidating interrogations.

Bayne, Pawlowski's lawyer, suggested that the Canadian Justice Department was being used by the Soviets as a "surrogate prosecutor." He said the Soviets were determined to get Pawlowski, because they considered him a traitor. Since they couldn't get their hands on him themselves, said Bayne, they were using the Canadian government to do the job for them. Bayne portrayed the Canadian prosecutors as dupes. "The Soviet tail," he maintained, "is wagging the democratic Canadian dog."

The judge's refusal to go along with the proposed commission was a big blow to the prosecution, but the war crimes unit decided to continue the case against Pawlowski. It sent another team to the Soviet Union to try to persuade the witnesses to come to Canada, and to seek more evidence against him. Meanwhile, procedural wrangling in the case continued, and the months ticked by.

The Crown tried to persuade Chadwick to remove himself from the case, hoping to find another judge who was not so opposed to commission evidence, and who might not have already formed opinions on the case. But Chadwick refused to step aside, and the Supreme Court of Canada backed him up on this. That sent the case back to Chadwick's courtroom, and set the stage for Round 2.

CHAPTER 23

Was it a KGB Plot?

More than a year had passed since Michael Pawlowski's arrest when he appeared again before Mr. Justice James Chadwick of the Ontario Supreme Court early in 1991. By that time, Imre Finta had been acquitted, and the case against a third war crimes suspect, Stephen Reistetter, was faltering.

The pressure was on the war crimes unit to win the Pawlowski case, but things just didn't seem to be going the Crown's way.

The death of a former Snov policeman named Sergiatitch Korolev, who was said by the Crown to have been crucial to its case, was billed as a big blow to the prosecution. But subsequent events were to show that if Korolev had lived to testify, he would not have turned out to be a damaging witness against Pawlowski.

Prosecutor James Sutton told Chadwick that Korolev's death in March 1991 made it necessary to drop four of the charges against Pawlowski. These were the charges involving the murders of 80 Poles near Yeskovichi and eight Jews at the Snov cemetery. Pawlowski remained charged with the murders of about 400 Jews outside of Snov and two Jewish women near the Snov cemetery.

Before the case was brought back before Chadwick, the war crimes unit and Pawlowski's lawyers went to Europe. The Crown tried to strengthen its position by lining up more witnesses, and trying to convince them to come to Canada to testify. The defence, meanwhile, was making some interesting discoveries which showed that the Soviets were playing less than straight with the Canadian investigators.

Sutton said that the loss of Korolev was not fatal to the Crown's case, and the number of witnesses against Pawlowski had increased from 12 to 15. They included five people who would be called upon to identify Pawlowski, along with three cart drivers and seven former police officers who would testify about various aspects of Pawlowski's alleged involvement in the murders.

The prosecutors had still been unable to persuade any of the European witnesses to come to Canada to testify, so the Crown once again applied to Chadwick for permission to send a commission to Belarus to videotape testimony, which would be presented to a jury in Canada. Once again, Chadwick turned the request down.

Chadwick's written judgment, which was released in June 1991, revealed what might have happened if the case had gone to trial. A jury would have likely found him not guilty. It would have been another defeat for the war crimes unit, and another example of the futility of trying to use a Canadian court to prosecute a suspect for things which allegedly happened in Europe half a century earlier.

Chadwick examined videotapes of witnesses, along with transcripts and other documents supplied by the Soviets. He was not impressed with what he saw. He discovered that the witnesses would present a flimsy case against Pawlowski, despite the fact that the team had spent three years getting those witnesses to testify.

Thanks to the investigation carried out by Pawlowski's defence lawyers when they went to Belarus, the judge also discovered the questionable nature of the Soviet documentary evidence. This supported defence attorney Donald Bayne's contention that the war crimes investigators were being fed false information by the Soviets in an attempt to prosecute an innocent man.

Chadwick expressed concern about evidence which was going to be used in an attempt to identify Pawlowski. In one photo spread shown to witnesses, there was the only one photo of a blond person, and since Pawlowski had light hair at the time the photo was taken, the witnesses not surprisingly picked him out. Chadwick also took note of an RCMP videotape made of one prospective witness, a woman named Anna Makavchik.

She told the Mounties that in 1985, she had been ordered by her employers to observe a man as he viewed a photograph of several people. The man had apparently died, and this was a round-about and dubious way of establishing Pawlowski's identity.

"I don't remember, actually," the woman said when asked if she recalled seeing the man identify Pawlowski's photograph. "I heard the name Plaska and Pawlowski, too," she said. But she said she didn't see the photograph herself, or appear to have any idea who Pawlowski was.

"It is obvious from the transcripts of all the identification witnesses," Chadwick concluded, "that the Crown is going to have some difficulty in the introduction of identification evidence on the commission and at trial."

The judge came down hard on Soviet investigative procedures, and the way in which the communists interrogated people. He cited a series of statements which had been taken by the Soviets from Korolev, who had been billed as the Crown's star witness until his death.

Korolev was initially questioned in 1949. The records showed that the interview lasted for more than two hours, but the transcript was only 1 ½ pages long, and was obviously incomplete. It contained only two questions and two answers. The next day, he was grilled for another two hours, but the result was just another 1 ½ pages, with four questions and four answers.

Canadian police procedures would have required all the questions and all the answers to have been recorded, so that the court could determine whether the statements were legally admissible as evidence. But that wasn't done by the Soviets in 1949, and it wasn't done again in 1970, 1979 and 1985, when they took more statements from him.

One session in 1985 lasted 7 ½ hours, and yet not a single question was recorded. The six-page transcript was used as the basis for the questioning of Korolev by the RCMP in 1989.

"It's obvious that at a criminal trial in Canada such statements would be highly questionable and in all probability not admissible," Chadwick said.

The judge was also concerned that the Soviets had withheld information which would have been to Pawlowski's advantage. This fact was uncovered by Pawlowski's defence team, who found the missing statements in West Germany.

"The Canadian investigators were not aware of all the previous statements given by the witnesses," the judge pointed out.

> In particular, the witness Korolev had given statements in 1970 and 1979 which were not produced by the Soviets but were discovered in a German archive. All of the statements

given by Korolev contradict each other. In fact, the 1970 and 1979 statements were done for the purpose of prosecuting other persons.

The 1970 statement was given in a case against two Germans who were accused of committing war crimes. It quoted Korolev as saying that the mass shooting of the Jews at Snov was carried out by these Germans, not the local police.

In the 1970 statement, Korolev said:

The Germans arrived at Snov early in the morning and cordoned off the village. Some of the Germans stood in the cordon while the others went from house to house and collected the Jews together regardless of sex and age on the village square, near the fire department. Some of the Jews were shot in their homes and on the street during the assembly.

One Jew, whose last name I do not know, jumped into a well and a German shot him there from a sub-machine gun. After assembly, the Jews were led out of town under guard to a clearing in the forest, about 2-3 km from Snov, where they were shot. The shooting was done in a pit which had been dug previously. The Germans themselves did the shooting, since only they went to the execution site.

But the 1979 statement was given for the purpose of prosecuting a local man who was the chief of police of Nesvizh, and it told a different story. This time, Korolev was quoted as putting the blame on the local police, as well as the Nazis. The local police chief is portrayed as the villain, and Pawlowski is not mentioned.

But Korolev's 1985 statement was taken by the Soviets for the purpose of showing that Pawlowski was a war criminal. It quoted Korolev as saying:

At the end of 1941 or the beginning of 1942, I don't remember exactly, Pavlovskiy Mikhail was appointed to the post of secretary of Snov police station. From the very beginning of his service in the police, Pavlovskiy (revealed) himself to be a zealous defender of the occupation regime established by the Hitlerites. He treated patriotically-inclined Soviet citizens with hatred, and initiated the extermination of peaceful citizens of Jewish and Polish nationality.

The 1985 statement went on to say:

All the policemen from Snov took part in the shooting of the Jews with the exception of one officer. I remember well that Pavlovskiy took an active part in the shooting of the Jews. Being among the policemen who were shooting, I personally saw him shooting people with his rifle. I can't say how many people he shot. The corpses of those who had been shot were buried by villagers from Panyutichi who had been assembled for that purpose.

Whether or not the man Korolev was referring to in this 1985 statement was Michael Pawlowski had not, of course, been established.

Chadwick went on to quote from an RCMP interview with Korolev on June 6, 1989. At that time, he said he did not remember how many times he had previously given statements regarding what happened in the Snov area during the war. The interview was conducted by Sgt. Richard Migras of the RCMP, who was attached to the war crimes unit.

When Migras asked him about the statement he had given to the Soviet interrogators in 1985, he responded: "I testified on the Pavlovskii affair, but I don't remember the contents of my testimony." Later, Migras asked him: "Did Pavlovskii take part in the shooting of this group of people?" Korolev replied: "It seems we were all there. I remember only poorly now, since a lot of time has gone by."

Chadwick summed up this part of his judgment by noting that there were two problems with the statements attributed to Korolev: they contradicted one another, and the Soviets withheld the statements which did not implicate Pawlowski.

"The question is raised as to the reliability of these statements and testimony," the judge concluded,

> especially in view of the fact that the Soviet authorities did not provide the 1970 and 1979 statements to the Canadian investigation team. The 1985 statement is contradictory to the 1970 and 1979 statements.

The judge noted that an expert on the Soviet legal system, Dr. Peter Solomon, had confirmed when questioned by Pawlowski's lawyers that the Soviets could not be trusted. Solomon said the Soviets had,

> a track record of many abuses as recently as the 1980s, which includes the 1986 to 1988 period. These abuses included suspects being interviewed repeatedly without any protection. This is with a view to trying to get them to confess. Also, investigators created cases improperly leading to the conviction of people later shown to be innocent.

Chadwick found that all but one of the crucial witnesses had been convicted as collaborationists after the war and sentenced by the Soviets to long jail terms. "They were subjected to torture in order to obtain confessions and received brief unfair trials," he said.

Chadwick said that transcripts of RCMP examinations of most of the elderly witnesses showed they had no clear recollection of the events, "and therefore their memory may need to be refreshed by the use of statements. The problem then arises as to what statement is used for the purpose of refreshing the memory." In some cases, these people didn't even remember giving statements, let alone what they had said in them. This, together with the fact that the people who had originally taken the statements were unavailable to testify, would make cross-examination of the witnesses almost impossible.

The judge concluded that it all added up to a potential violation of Pawlowski's rights, under the Charter of Rights and Freedoms. The accused man would not be able to make a proper answer and defence to the charges, as he had a right to, under the Charter. On that basis, Chadwick refused the Crown's application to send a commission to Belarus to videotape evidence. That, for all intents and purposes, was the end of the case, but the war crimes unit refused to give up. The prosecution tried to have Chadwick's ruling overturned. Early in 1992, the Supreme Court of Canada refused leave to appeal, and after that the Crown dropped the case against Pawlowski.

"I feel great," he said, "because I was innocent at the beginning, and for 2 ½ years I have suffered, for what? That's really shameful."

Bayne, his lawyer, said that "a perfectly innocent man has been vilified as a major war criminal." He put the blame for that on political pressure which had been applied to the government to go after suspected war criminals, and on the Soviets for trumping up false evidence against Pawlowski. "There was no question the KGB and Soviets did not like Michael Pawlowski," Bayne said. "They never forgot – they wanted to punish Michael."

Bayne said he was suspicious of the fact that Korolev, "who was going to be a great embarrassment to the KGB," died just two months after speaking to the defence team. Bayne said that Korolev had admitted that he fabricated his allegations against Pawlowski in 1985, and that he wanted to tell the Canadians that his statement was untrue. "In 1990," Bayne said, "we interviewed Korolev and he told us it was a totally manufactured effort. . . . Pawlowski wasn't there."

Chadwick took the unusual step of awarding Pawlowski almost $151,000 to help cover his legal costs. This was on top of $55,000 which the government had already paid to him.

The dropping of the charges against Pawlowski sparked angry reactions from spokesmen for Jewish groups. Some accused Canadian judges of being too concerned with the rights of suspected war criminals, and too quick to dismiss the suffering of the Jews in the Holocaust.

Others said the war crimes unit just didn't have any fire in its belly.

CHAPTER 24

A Postcard Did Him In

One day in November 1992, a balding, bespectacled 73-year-old man tripped and fell as he walked through a Vancouver office building. Journalists who had been stalking the old man moved in quickly, recognizing the symbolic value of the occasion. The old man had indeed taken a great fall.

After a tense, five-year legal battle with the federal government, Jacob Luitjens was finally going to be deported to start serving a prison sentence in Holland. On national television that night, Canadians saw him sprawled on the floor, clutching his fedora in his right hand, struggling to regained his feet and his dignity.

Some people felt sorry for the feeble old man and thought it was ridiculous to go after him for crimes he committed when he was in his 20s. But others were delighted that Luitjens was finally going to get what was coming to him. They hoped he would be locked up in a Dutch jail and kept there for the rest of his life.

When Luitjens was a young man in Holland during the Second World War, he was a collaborator. He bullied his fellow-citizens, broke into their homes in the middle of the night and told the Nazis which people were Jews.

After the war, he ran away to South America, and eventually came to Canada. He settled in Vancouver, earned a university degree, got a good job, bought a house, raised his children, took out Canadian citizenship, and wisely avoided going back to the old country for a vacation. Like hundreds of other alleged Nazi war criminals who came to Canada, Jacob Luitjens thought he had put his past behind him.

Unlike most of the others, Luitjens got caught.

He was born in 1919 in what is now Indonesia. It was a Dutch colony, and like most of the Europeans who lived there, the Luitjens family were right-wingers. As a boy, Jacob picked up the nickname of Jaap. When he was four years old, the family moved to Holland. His father, a veterinarian, set up a practice in Roden, a small town in northern Holland. Jacob finished elementary and secondary school, then began studying law at the University of Groeningen.

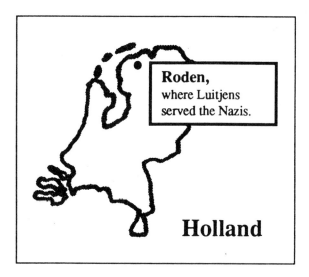

Roden, where Luitjens served the Nazis.

Holland

When the Dutch army surrendered to the Nazis in 1940, most of the people in Roden didn't like it, but the Luitjens family thought it was a step forward, and they welcomed the oppressors. The father and his children were anti-Semites and Nazi sympathizers. Jacob, his older brother Piet, and their father all joined the Dutch National Socialist Movement, which later became the Dutch Nazi Party. Jacob also joined the Landwacht, a military-style police unit which was like the Nazi SS.

He wore a black uniform and carried a pistol and a shotgun. He was in his early 20s at the time, and claimed later that he joined these groups not so much because he liked the Nazis, but because he was against the communists, and this was a good way to fight them. But his fellow-citizens feared and hated Luitjens and others like him. They called the Landwacht "the blood squad" and "the

quisling militia." Some of the townspeople had a nickname for
Luitjens. They called him the "holy terror of Roden."

Luitjens wasn't a full-time bully and traitor. He continued going
to university, but spent a good part of his time working with the
Nazis to identify Jews and oppress his countrymen.

When Holland was liberated in 1945, Luitjens surrendered to
the authorities. He spent about 18 months in detention camps and
prisons. Conditions were poor, but at least Luitjens was alive.
Many others who had helped the Nazis were executed by the
Resistance, or given long prison sentences by Dutch courts.
Luitjens was scheduled to go on trial in 1947, but in late 1946 he
fled to a German refugee camp.

He posed as a displaced person from East Prussia who had fled
the advancing Russian army in 1945. He used the name of Gerhard
Harder, and he claimed to be a Mennonite. In 1948 the Mennonite
church arranged for "Harder" to travel by ship to South America.
He ended up in Paraguay, which was governed by fascists and
welcomed Nazi war criminals.

Meanwhile, his case finally came up in court in the Netherlands,
despite the fact that he was no longer in Dutch custody. He was
tried in his absence, convicted and sentenced to life imprisonment
for aiding and abetting the enemy. He was one of many who were
found guilty of such crimes. A large number of people in Holland
had collaborated with the enemy, and about 66,000 Dutch citizens
were eventually convicted of war crimes. Since Luitjens had disappeared, his prison sentence remained unserved, but his conviction stayed on the books.

But Luitjens wasn't worried. He was safe in Paraguay – safe
enough to feel free to drop the alias of Gerhard Harder and resume
using his own name. He learned Spanish, taught elementary and
secondary school, got married to a woman named Olga Klassen,
had three children, and became a baptized member of the Mennonite church. It looked like he had escaped from Dutch justice.

If he had stayed in South America, he almost certainly would
never have been caught and punished for his war crimes. But he
decided to go to Canada, where his wife's parents were already
living, and where he thought he could have an even better life than
the one he was living in Paraguay. Ultimately, that decision to
move to Canada was his undoing.

Luitjens and his wife and children arrived in Vancouver in 1961.
They were sponsored as immigrants by his wife's parents, who had

moved to Canada from Holland in 1956. Luitjens filled out a routine immigration form and lied about his past. He was required to list his previous addresses, and he lied about that, omitting the fact that he had been detained in Dutch prison camps after the war. The form also asked if he had a criminal record. He lied about that too, failing to report his conviction in Holland for treason.

If he had disclosed the truth about his background, his application for admission to Canada would have been rejected. But because he lied, and because immigration officials had no efficient way to detect such deceptions, Luitjens managed to slip into Canada.

He got into the country easily, on the strength of his sponsorship by his wife's parents, despite the fact that he was a convicted Nazi war criminal, and despite the fact that his name appeared on lists of wanted persons which were circulated by the Dutch government.

Once he was admitted to Canada, Luitjens thought he was home free. He kept silent about what he had done in the war, and set about making a good life for himself and his family. He earned a bachelor of arts degree and got a job teaching botany at the University of British Columbia. He applied for Canadian citizenship and he received it in 1971, after lying again on his application form.

He also lied about his past during an interview which was required before his citizenship was granted. It was easy once again for him to get away with it. Nobody suspected that there was anything in his distant past which might disqualify him from Canadian citizenship.

For the next 10 years, Luitjens kept a low profile and enjoyed the benefits and privileges of Canadian citizenship. He kept working at the university, and avoided talking about what he had done during the war. But in 1981, Luitjens made a mistake.

He sent a postcard to his father back in the old country. His proud father showed the card to a postman, boasting that his son was doing well in Canada. It was a foolish thing to do, in view of the fact that Jacob Luitjens was still a wanted man, even though his conviction for treason stretched back 33 years, to 1948.

The postman happened to mention to somebody that Jacob Luitjens, the one-time Terror Of Roden, was living comfortably in Vancouver. Word got around that the unpunished war criminal was living the good life in Canada, and eventually the information made its way to a Dutch journalist named Sjoerd Post.

Post had written a series of articles about war criminals for his newspaper. After those articles were published, he received an anonymous telephone call from a man suggesting that he try and track down Jacob Luitjens. By that point the story had become garbled. The tipster told Post that Luitjens could be in Paraguay, Argentina or Canada.

Playing a long-shot, Post asked a colleague who was going to Canada to try to find Luitjens. Post's colleague ended up in Vancouver, and when he looked in the phone book, he saw the name of Jacob Luitjens, who was making no effort to disguise his real identity.

Post's colleague contacted Luitjens, who was friendly at first, glad to talk to someone from the old country. But alarm bells went off when the journalist started to ask Luitjens about what he had done during the war. When he was asked flat out if he was the same Jacob Luitjens who had collaborated with the Nazis during the war, and if he realized he had been convicted *in absentia* by a Dutch court in 1948, Luitjens replied, "No, I never heard that." Then he slammed the door in the reporter's face.

Sjoerd Post and his colleagues in the Dutch news media made headlines with the news that Luitjens was an unpunished war criminal living in Vancouver. The story was picked up by Canadian newspapers and television. Soon there were demands by Jewish activists and others that the Canadian government take action against this Nazi war criminal.

This was not the first time something like this had happened. In previous years, there had been many reports in the news media about suspected Nazi war criminals in Canada, but the government had consistently refused to take legal action against them. The same thing happened in this case, and after a week or so, the whole thing blew over and Luitjens quietly continued his life in Canada.

But a couple of years later, another Dutch reporter named Alphonsus van Westerloo picked up the story, and he managed to interview Luitjens in Vancouver. The fact that Luitjens was willing to talk to van Westerloo is a good indication of how safe he felt in Canada, and how confident he was that the Canadian government was not going to try and deport him. In his interview with van Westerloo, Luitjens tried to explain away his past.

"As a young student in those days I was ambitious to build a better world," Luitjens told the reporter. "I chose the wrong path."

He tried to minimize his guilt by claiming that "both sides committed crimes," and even made a pitch for sympathy. "They are now playing cat and mouse with me," he complained. "Occasionally they loosen the strings and then they tighten them up again."

The interview that Luitjens gave to van Westerloo generated another flurry of media publicity in both Holland and Canada. There were cries of outrage and disgust from Jewish groups, war veterans and others that a convicted Nazi war criminal could continue to live in Canada. There were demands that the government do something about it, but the Canadian authorities still failed to act against Luitjens.

In 1983, at age 64, Luitjens left his job as an instructor at the university, and he embarked upon what he hoped would be a pleasant and peaceful retirement. He lived in a small white house in a working-class area of east Vancouver, raised pigeons as a hobby and hoped everyone would forget about what he had done during the war.

But the Dutch authorities persisted. They formally requested that the Canadian government extradite Luitjens. Ottawa turned them down on the grounds that the extradition treaty between Canada and Holland didn't cover the crime for which Luitjens had been convicted. He had been convicted of aiding and abetting the enemy, the Canadians pointed out, and that wasn't one of the offences which was specified in the treaty.

The Dutch government responded by asking Canada to agree to amend the treaty, which dated back to 1899 and which was due for review and updating. Once again Ottawa found a way to avoid the issue. Ottawa responded that the time was not right to amend the treaty. Frustrated Dutch government officials understandably concluded that for some reason, the Canadian government was always going to find an excuse for not extraditing Luitjens.

In 1985, they decided that public pressure might accomplish what quiet diplomacy had been unable to accomplish. The Dutch decided to appeal directly to the Canadian public. Dutch Ambassador Naboth van Dijl called in the news media.

"We have been trying to get Jacob Luitjens extradited for years," van Dijl announced, "but there was no way to do it because the crime for which he was convicted in the Netherlands is not mentioned in the treaty between the two countries." The ambassador explained why the Dutch government still wanted to bring Luitjens to justice.

Put on the spot by van Dijl, Justice Minister John Crosbie was forced to respond publicly. But once again, he tried to duck the issue. He told reporters the crime Luitjens had been convicted of – aiding and abetting the enemy – was the same thing as treason. "We are not going to amend the treaty to include treason," Crosbie explained, "because it is a political offence, and it isn't customary for extradition treaties to deal with the subject of treason."

Once again it looked like Luitjens was safe, thanks to the Canadian government's stubborn persistence in following a do-nothing policy when it came to bringing Nazi war criminals in Canada to justice. But meanwhile, other events were unfolding. Publicity surrounding the Luitjens case and several others which had arisen over the years forced the government to appoint a commission of inquiry into the whole war criminals issue.

The man who headed that inquiry, Jules Deschênes, submitted his report to the government in 1986. In that report, Deschênes probably listed Luitjens as one of 20 Nazi war criminals in Canada who required "urgent attention." The names on the list were kept secret.

Finally, in early 1988, Ottawa took action. The government decided to strip Luitjens of his Canadian citizenship, paving the way for his deportation to Holland. Luitjens was given notice by the Secretary of State of Canada that the federal Cabinet intended to revoke his citizenship. Luitjens was told that he had the legal right to request that a Federal Court judge hear evidence in the matter. Luitjens exercised his right to go to court.

Mr. Justice Frank Collier of the Federal Court of Canada was appointed to hear the case. Collier started hearing evidence in September 1988. The judge listened to evidence in Vancouver, then went to Holland to hear more evidence, and finished up by holding more sessions in Vancouver. The testimony was taken intermittently over an eight-month period. It was a long, slow procedure, but when it was over it was clear that the prosecution had made a strong case in favor of stripping Luitjens of his Canadian citizenship.

The government's case was helped by the fact that even though so many years had passed, a lot of people in Holland still remembered Luitjens, and were willing to testify against him. They had grown up with him in the town of Roden, which had only about 1,200 people. He was also easy to remember because he was a very good-looking young man, and because he had a deformed left hand. His hand had virtually no fingers, and only a thumb.

He was also memorable because he had worked for the Nazis for almost five years, and he had hurt a lot of people. Many of them were still around.

One woman who gave evidence was Riemkje Stall. She recalled the night that Luitjens and other members of the Landwacht broke into her family's house and questioned her about some identity papers. When Luitjens didn't like her answers, she remembered vividly, "he slapped me in the face."

Roelf Meyer, who had played with Luitjens as a child, recalled that Luitjens came to his home and helped arrest his 72-year-old father. Another witness, Dirk Kok, was only nine years old when Luitjens helped arrest his father, but he remembered it well. "I will never forget that face," Kok told the judge.

Collier also heard about the time that Luitjens helped the Germans chase down a Resistance man named Henni Jensen, who was shot and killed. And then there was the time Luitjens helped the Nazis find a deserter from the German navy, who also died of a gunshot wound.

Luitjens took the witness stand in his own defence. He admitted being part of the Nazi collaborationist police force, but minimized the brutality he had used. He claimed he was unable to recall many of the details about what had happened so many years earlier.

He also testified that converting to Christianity after the war was the most important thing in his life. He said he knew that God forgave him for helping the Nazis against his fellow-countrymen.

"Seeing my life through the eyes of God is more terrible than any court can be," he told the judge. "My whole life is like a film and I see it through God's eyes . . . you capitulate totally and say God has forgiven me."

When the testimony was finished, Collier reserved judgment on the case. He took an unusually long time to reach his decision, and explained later that he had difficulty making up his mind on some of the complex legal issues which the case raised. It was the first time the Canadian government had taken action against a suspected war criminal by trying to denaturalize him. Collier sat on the case for a very long time. He didn't release his judgment for almost two and a half years.

Finally, in October 1991, he ruled that the government had succeeded in proving that Luitjens had obtained his Canadian citizenship "by false representation or by knowingly concealing material circumstances." The judge said he believed the witnesses who testified against Luitjens, while he found Luitjens to be less than credible. "In cross-examination," the judge observed, "he was often evasive, unresponsive and hedging." He said he suspected that Luitjens had used the legal training he got during the war to come up with ways to avoid admitting the truth.

After the judge's ruling, the federal cabinet was able to act. It went ahead and denaturalize Luitjens, but that wasn't the end the matter. Luitjens still had rights, even though he was no longer a Canadian citizen. When he was served with a notice that the government intended to deport him, he was once again entitled to his day in court.

This time the case was heard by an Immigration Department official. Much of the same ground was covered as had been gone over in the Federal Court trial. Once again, Luitjens lost.

The end of Luitjens long struggle to remain in Canada was finally near. On that day in November 1992 when Luitjens tripped and fell in front of the news cameras, he was on his way to his final Immigration Department hearing. He had exhausted all his legal rights to appeal. On November 26, 1992, he was deported from Canada.

When the plane carrying Luitjens touched down in Holland, it was another big day for the news media. The landing and the quick arrest of Luitjens by Dutch police was carried live on Dutch TV. It wasn't every day that a man who had committed war crimes almost half a century earlier was brought home to face punishment.

He was taken to jail. Luitjens was finally to start paying for the crimes he had committed so many years earlier.

The following month, when he appealed in a Dutch court for a new trial, he said: "I regret that at that time I had an ideology which I did not know would finally lead to the murder of so many people." The court turned down his appeal, and he returned to jail.

Luitjens continued to collect his pension cheques from the University of British Columbia and government of Canada. His life sentence was commuted and he was released from prison in March 1995 at the age of 75, after spending 28 months behind bars.

He applied for re-admission to Canada, but Ottawa turned him down. Having gone to so much trouble to kick him out of the country, the authorities weren't about to let him back in.

CHAPTER 25

His Prayers Were Answered

Stephen Reistetter was a true believer.

He went to mass almost every day at St. Julia's Roman Catholic Church in St. Catharines, Ontario. On the day in January 1990 when he was arrested on war crimes charges, the 75-year-old man asked God to help him prove his innocence.

His alleged legal sins dated back 48 years. They were said to have been committed in 1942 in Slovakia, which was independent of Czechoslovakia during the war. Reistetter was accused of being responsible for the forced deportation of some 3,000 Slovakian Jews, but he insisted he wasn't involved.

Reistetter was the third person to be charged with committing war crimes under the Criminal Code. Jewish groups were encouraged by Reistetter's arrest, which came just a month after Michael Pawlowski's, and while Imre Finta was still on trial. The Jews were hoping that the Justice Department's war crimes unit was finally getting its act together, but that didn't turn out to be the case.

While the Justice Department expressed confidence in the strength of its case, the truth was that the war crimes unit and the RCMP were desperately scrambling to come up with compelling evidence against him.

They were caught in a bind. If they waited much longer, they feared that Reistetter might die or become too ill to be put on trial. But they simply weren't ready to bring him to trial, so they charged him and gambled that they could find enough evidence against him to win a conviction by the time he went before a jury.

Reistetter immigrated to Canada in the late 1940s. The fact that he was an official in a political party with ties to the Nazis didn't prevent him from getting into Canada. In fact, his staunch anti-communism was likely considered to be in Reistetter's favor. He settled in St. Catharines, a city of about 130,000 in the Niagara Peninsula, got a job with General Motors, and worked for the automaker until his retirement in 1980.

In his younger years, he was active in the Slovakian-Canadian community, which opposed the communists who took power in their homeland after the war. In his later years, Reistetter became increasingly devout and involved with the Roman Catholic Church. But despite the fact that he was a good Christian and a God-fearing man, his arrest came as no surprise.

He had been dogged by war crimes allegations for a long time, and in 1985 he appeared before the Deschênes commission for two days of secret testimony concerning what had gone on in Slovakia during the war. That same year, he was publicly identified as a possible war criminal by "the fifth estate," a CBC television program. The program linked Reistetter to the deportation of the Jews and alleged that he was "a person of influence" in the Hlinka party, which was in power in Slovakia during the war, and had close ties to the Nazis.

The Slovakian government deported thousands of Jews as part of a "resettling" program. The stated purpose was to give the Jews new homes in Poland, but in fact they were sent by the Nazis to the extermination camp at Auschwitz. When this was revealed, the Slovakian government stopped sending Jews to Poland.

Reistetter denied any part in the deportations. He maintained that as a Hlinka party secretary in the Bardejov district, he was only concerned with economic and cultural matters, not government activities. Reistetter accused the CBC of being unable to distinguish between government activity and local party activity. Said Reistetter:

> To accuse me of responsibility for the deportation of and confiscation of property from Jews is absolutely absurd and false. It is like the secretary of the Liberal or Conservative parties in St. Catharines being responsible for the things done by the federal government.

Five years later, after he was arrested, several people rushed to his defence, including his next-door neighbor. Helen Stewart recalled how helpful Reistetter and his wife had been after Stewart's

husband died. "They were the first ones to come over here," she recalled, "and if anything else was wrong, or if I ever needed any help, they were the first ones here."

Reistetter and his wife were married in 1941, the year before his alleged war crimes. Mary Reistetter said her husband "never, never" did what the prosecutors accused him of doing. "He helped people in his village," she maintained. "If someone was in trouble, he would help them. Ever since I married him, I don't know of him doing anything wrong."

Reistetter was wearing handcuffs when he was brought into the Ontario Supreme Court in Toronto the day after he was arrested. It was the first time he had ever been before a judge, and he looked bewildered. He wore a plaid shirt with a tie and a sports jacket, and he had hearing aids in both ears. His bail was set at $100,000, but since he couldn't come up with the money immediately, he spent a couple of nights in the Don Jail.

His lawyer, John Stephens, said Reistetter was eager to have the trial begin, so he could prove his client's innocence in court. "All he can do right now is maintain his innocence and wait until his trial," said Stephens, as he walked beside his client up the ramp from the Don Jail's basement, after Reistetter's family had posted bail. At the time, Stephens was unaware that the war crimes unit was not interested in going to trial quickly, because it did not have enough evidence against Reistetter.

The Crown looked like it was getting off to a good start when it managed to persuade Mr. Justice Douglas Carruthers of the Ontario Supreme Court that an evidence-gathering commission should be sent to Czechoslovakia to videotape testimony. Government lawyer Arnold Fradkin said that the commission should go soon, because the four witnesses whose evidence was to be video-taped were not well, and the man who was supposed to be the key witness among them had already suffered three strokes.

What was not discussed in open court was why the war crimes unit was only now seeking permission to videotape the evidence. Since Reistetter had been suspected of war crimes since at least 1985, why had the prosecutors not gone out and gathered their videotape evidence previously? Why had they laid the charges first, and then decided that they needed to take their cameras to Czecho-slovakia to record the testimony?

The case took another strange twist a few months later. Fradkin asked Carruthers to approve the sending of a second videotaping commission to Czechoslovakia. Fradkin claimed that investigators had found more witnesses to testify against Reistetter, and said he needed a second judicially-sanctioned videotaping team to go over-seas to record their evidence.

Carruthers was once again agreeable. This pleased the war crimes unit, which was having trouble getting another judge to go along with the idea of videotaping evidence in the Michael Pawlowski case (see Chapters 22-23). The five new witnesses in the Reistetter case, plus the four others who had already given their evidence on tape, were only part of what sounded like a strong case for the prosecution. Fradkin said that about 15 additional witnesses would be travelling to Toronto to testify against Reistet-ter when he came up for trial.

This was the last the public heard about the case until March 1991, when Reistetter was ordered to appear in court so a trial date could be set. Reistetter went to his church in St. Catharines that morning, as usual, before taking the 90-minute bus trip to Toronto to learn when he was going to be put on trial.

But in a stunning about-face, the Crown dropped the charges against Reistetter. It was a sudden and unexpected end to the case. Everything that had been said up to that point by the prosecution had made it look like the case against Reistetter was strong, and that it was going to trial.

Why did the government suddenly throw in the towel?

Fradkin offered no comment, but Justice Department lawyer Gilles Renaud said that the two evidence-gathering trips to Czechoslovakia "didn't advance the Crown's case as expected." He said that the man who was supposed to be the Crown's key witness had died, and so the prosecution had to be abandoned. That was the explanation which was carried in the news media at the time, and it's the same one which is generally given when the case is referred to in the media to this day.

In fact, it's a phony excuse for a poor job of prosecution. The "star witness" who died turned out to be nothing more than a historian. He was going to give evidence about the political situation in Slovakia during the war, and would have attempted to link the Hlinka party and Reistetter to the government of the day, which was responsible for the deportations. It has never been explained why another historian could not have been used, or why this particular expert in history was so vital to the Crown's case.

Renaud said that another witness was too ill to testify, and a third one – who was said to have supplied the key information which led the government to lay the charges against Reistetter – had refused to testify. This, too, was left unexplained. Why did this witness suddenly change his mind about giving evidence? What information had he initially provided? Why did the war crimes unit rely on this unreliable witness when it decided to lay the charges against Reistetter? More unanswered questions.

And what about the remaining witnesses? Renaud admitted that "an important part of their testimony relied on hearsay." In other words, it was evidence which likely would not have been admissible in court.

Defence attorney Stephens said he suspected that the government's supposedly-solid case was a sham when the prosecutors wouldn't go along with his request that the case be brought to trial quickly. Stephens said that the prosecution's case was so shabby that one of the Crown's best witnesses had turned out to be quite favorable toward Reistetter.

Stephens also wondered why the death of the historian, who was supposed to be the Crown's strongest witness, had been billed as a fatal blow to the prosecution's case. He pointed out that the historian's evidence had already been videotaped, so his death did not mean the Crown could not use his evidence.

Reistetter, surprised that he was let go on the day he thought he was going to learn his trial date, climbed on a bus in Toronto and enjoyed the ride home to St. Catharines. When he got there, he told reporters that he was not bitter about being falsely accused, but he wished that he had been given his day in court, so he could have proven his innocence.

But the most important thing, he said, was to offer his thanks to God for his deliverance. He went to his church, where friends soon gathered to congratulate him. "Our prayers," said Father Fred Colli, his parish priest, "have been answered."

Reistetter said "Amen" to that.

CHAPTER 26

He Worked For the RCMP

The war crimes unit launched its fourth and final criminal prosecution in late 1992. It was the strangest one of them all.

The suspect was a Serbian immigrant named Radislav Grujicic who had worked as a spy for the RCMP, despite the fact that the Mounties were well aware of his activities during the war. When Grujicic's involvement with the federal police force came to light, the judge threw the case out of court.

The judge blasted the government for waiting so long to prosecute him, when it had known for decades that Grujicic had been wanted by the Yugoslavian government on war crimes charges. If what Grujicic had done was so terrible, the judge asked, why had the government waited until he was a sick old man in his 80s before bringing him to court.

Grujicic was picked up by his former employers on December 8, 1992. Five Mounties showed up at the senior citizens' home in Windsor, Ontario, where he lived. He was so old and sick that at first, he thought his old friends from the RCMP had come to pay a social call.

Grujicic, who was 81 years old, had to be physically supported by a Mountie when he made his first appearance in court later that day. It was symbolic, since the Mounties had been quietly supporting Grujicic for more than 40 years. Now they were turning on their old underground operative.

Grujicic, who wore thick glasses and had a reputation for crankiness, suffered from diabetes and heart disease. As he stood

trembling before the judge, it was hard to understand what purpose was being served by prosecuting him. After three failures in
a row, it looked as if the war crimes unit was desperate to nail
somebody, and Grujicic looked like an easy target.

But even Sol Littman of the Simon Wiesenthal Centre was
dubious about prosecuting a suspected war criminal at this late
stage of his life. Littman had been told that Grujicic was suffering
from cancer of the prostate.

"I cannot tell whether the information is accurate or was intended to mislead me," Littman said in a letter to Justice Minister
Kim Campbell a few days after the charges were laid,

> but it would be wise to be sure before proceeding further. No
> matter how eager we are to see war criminals punished, our
> own sense of justice mitigates against subjecting a man who
> may be near death to the rigors of a trial.

Grujicic's past was not revealed immediately. It was buried in
the files of the RCMP and the Canadian Security and Intelligence
Service (CSIS). Initially, the court was told only that he had been
a senior official of the Belgrade police during the war. He was said
to have conspired with the pro-Nazi Serbian government and the
Germans in the classification, arrest and interrogation of communists, "resulting in their being killed." Specifically, he was charged
with 10 counts of murdering communists. There were also charges
of kidnapping and conspiracy to commit murder.

There was no mention of Jews. It was the first time since the
Luitjens case that a person accused of war crimes had appeared in
a Canadian court without being charged specifically with crimes
which were committed against Jews.

The story of Grujicic's long and complex life could fill a book, but
a lot more research needs to be done. Enough is now known,
however, to piece together some of the highlights.

Grujicic was born in a Serbian area of Montenegro. Early in his
life, he developed a strong sense of Serbian nationalism and devo-
tion to the Orthodox Church, which was strongly anti-communist.
He was an intelligent man, and studied law before becoming a
police officer in the Serbian capital of Belgrade during the early
years of the Second World War.

He collaborated with the Nazis when they arrived in Serbia in
1941, and was involved in the operation of a prison camp known
as Banjica just outside Belgrade. Banjica was notorious as a
torture and execution centre.

Grujicic was convicted of war crimes by the post-war communist government in 1947 and sentenced to death. But he was tried *in absentia*, since the Yugoslavians didn't know where he was. In fact, he was working for U.S. intelligence in Austria and Italy, helping the Americans identify suspected communists. After that, the Americans helped him immigrate to Canada, providing him with fake identification and a cover story.

He arrived in Halifax by ship from Genoa in August 1948, passing himself off as a displaced person. He had fake identification papers in the name of Marko Jankovic, and he settled in Toronto. It didn't take him long to find a job. He was soon hired by the RCMP to spy on left-wing Serbian, Croatian and Macedonian immigrants in the Toronto area. Grujicic was paid $100 month, which was a fair amount of money at the time.

He worked for the RCMP until 1951, when his true identity and background were exposed in a tabloid newspaper *Flash*. The headline of the story said: "Nazi-collaborator, brutal killer hides in Toronto under false name." Grujicic was so upset about being exposed that he went to the newspaper office and confronted the editor. That ended his usefulness to the RCMP as a secret agent.

After the Yugoslavian government made a formal request for his extradition, the Justice and Immigration departments asked the Mounties to look into the allegations that he was a war criminal. The Mounties lied to cover up for their man, saying that it was a case of mistaken identity, and that Jankovic was not Grujicic.

In the mid-1950s, Grujicic had no trouble gaining Canadian citizenship. Over the next several years, he moved around quite a bit, still pretending to be Jankovic and perhaps still working for the Mounties. He travelled back and forth between Canada and the United States several times, and may also have worked for the FBI. Both the RCMP and the FBI are known to have employed many informants to help them keep track of communists.

In 1969, Canadian immigration officials asked the RCMP about Grujicic again, after receiving another request from Yugoslavia that he be returned to his homeland to be punished for his war crimes. Once again, the Mounties lied to protect Grujicic. It had been 18 years since the previous inquiry, but the Mounties still protected him, as well as themselves. The deception was aided by the fact that the government at that time wasn't interested in pursuing war criminals in Canada.

It wasn't until the mid-1980s that the RCMP finally started coming clean about Grujicic. By that point, government policy had changed, and efforts were finally being made to bring war criminals in Canada to justice. Grujicic's name was among the hundreds which were submitted to the Deschênes commission. The war crimes unit began investigating him in 1989, and three years later, he was arrested.

Ivan Whitehall, the Justice Department's top lawyer, was in charge of the prosecution. Whitehall had represented the department as chief counsel before the Deschênes commission, and so he was familiar with the Grujicic case. Whitehall said he had 10 eye-witnesses lined up against Grujicic, and more were expected to come forward before the case went to trial.

Soon after Grujicic's arrest, the head of the war crimes unit, Peter Kremer, announced that 20 other "priority cases" were under way. Kremer said he hoped charges would be laid against some of these suspects soon. It was a familiar refrain. The war crimes unit, eager to justify its existence and its $3-million annual budget, seemed to be always making promises it didn't keep and predictions which didn't come true.

By mid-1983, the Grujicic case was bogged down in procedural wrangling. Defence lawyer Sam Vucinic complained about the lack of co-operation he was receiving from the prosecution. Eventually he was given about 30 boxes of documents, but the government refused to identify its witnesses or arrange a trip to Yugoslavia so the defence team could question witnesses.

In early 1994, Justice Department lawyers went to Budapest to videotape evidence from 17 witnesses. Budapest was chosen because of political problems in the former Yugoslavia. Whitehall said he still hoped that most of the witnesses would testify in person, and called the videotaping "insurance," in case some of the witnesses died or fell ill.

Meanwhile, Grujicic's health was getting worse, and the trial was delayed as the judge heard evidence on the suspect's fitness to stand trial. While this was going on, Grujicic often dozed off during the drawn-out court proceedings. He also needed frequent bathroom breaks, as medical witnesses testified in great detail about the state of Grujicic's health. It was obvious that the old man was sick, and in May he suffered a heart attack at his senior citizens' apartment. In August his condition got even worse. His right leg was amputated below the knee after gangrene set in.

On September 27, 1994, Mr. Justice William Donnelly said that enough was enough. He brought the prosecution of Grujicic to an end. The judge spent almost three hours talking about the case, revealing some of the details about what had gone on in Grujicic's life in Yugoslavia, in Europe after the war and in Canada.

He also reviewed the medical evidence and criticized the government for its failure to prosecute Grujicic earlier. "Federal authorities have known of the allegations against the accused since 1951," Donnelly pointed out.

> For 42 years, Canada not only took no action by deportation or extradition, but used the accused so long as he was useful, protected him long after his usefulness had passed, and granted him full rights as a citizen.

The judge called the Banjica prison camp "a spectre in horror." He said Serbian communists "were stripped of all rights, deprived of every vestige of humanity and reduced to numerical abstractions categorized for extermination or deportation to labor camps."

Prisoners were often killed in reprisal for actions against the Nazis by the Serbian resistance. "Implementation was immediate, ruthless and well publicized in order to terrorize and subjugate a conquered people," the judge said. He cited a case in 1943 in which four German soldiers were killed by partisans. Some 400 prisoners from Banjica were shot in reprisal. The 1942 annual report from Banjica to the Belgrade City Police shows that of the 7,992 people who entered the camp, 1,430 were shot, 1,130 went to forced labor in Germany, and 747 went to forced labor elsewhere.

The judge revealed an RCMP memo which spoke about "Radislav GRUJICICH – name changed February 1948 in Enns, Austria. U.S. authorization 480." This was evidence that the

Mounties knew who "Yankovic" really was, and that he had been given a fake identity by the Americans after he spied for them.

Another memo showed that Grujicic was hired by the RCMP in 1949. Written by Corporal W.D. Fast, the memo said "Marko Yankovich" was the former chief of the anti-communist section of the Belgrade political police. "It was obvious that Yankovich was well qualified for investigations in the subversive field, and his European police experience and political knowledge places him in a position which will prove of inestimable value to the Force," the memo continued.

> In addition, he is already acquainted with some of the left-wing
> Serbian, Croatian and Macedonian elements, particularly
> those who have had questionable political records in
> Yugoslavia and migrated to this country.

Grujicic apparently stopped working for the Mounties when he was exposed by *Flash* in 1951, but a memo written in 1969 by W.L. Higgitt, who at the time was head of security and intelligence and later became RCMP commissioner, showed that the Mounties were still covering up. In that memo, written in reply to an inquiry from immigration officials, Higgitt said: "No developments have occurred which would cause any change in our belief of mistaken identity."

The judge, obviously disgusted with the way the war crimes unit and the RCMP handled the Grujicic case, concluded: "I have no sense that justice is being done, or is being seen to be done." With that, the prosecution of Grujicic ended.

By that point, he was beyond caring. Grujicic had been transferred to a nursing home to live out his final days.

Some Final Cases

Michael Pawlowski

CHAPTER 27

The Morgue Monster

One Nazi war criminal who immigrated to Canada got a job as a morgue attendant. He was good at his work because he was so accustomed to being around human corpses.

He was a former German soldier identified only as "Felix," and he coldly admitted, without expressing the slightest remorse, that he had murdered many Jews and gypsies in Eastern Europe during the war.

But Felix was not so bad, according to his former employer, an Ottawa physician and pathologist named Dr. Douglas Waugh, who described Felix as "a cherubic innocent with an almost childlike acceptance of just one more of the vagaries of human existence."

Noting that Felix was a peasant who came from the German province of Silesia, Waugh said:

> Certainly he showed none of the ideological overlay I might
> have expected in a former member of Hitler's legions. He was
> just a simple farmer doing to humans what he'd always done
> to farm animals.

The pathologist said he found Felix to be "a superb morgue attendant, one of the best in an occupation not noted for charming role models and mentors. His work was meticulous."

Waugh described Felix in an article the *Canadian Medical Association Journal*. After the article was published in the April 1993 edition, there was an outcry from the Jewish community, which demanded that Felix be identified, arrested and prosecuted as a war criminal.

But Waugh refused to reveal Felix's real name, even when he was questioned by the RCMP. The doctor said he was "embarrassed to have put him in the public eye."

Waugh said he didn't consider Felix to be a war criminal, but rather "as much a victim of his acts as those he killed."

Waugh, a former executive director of the Association of Canadian Medical Colleges, said Felix told him about the wartime murders one day while the two men were at work in the morgue.

"We had a sad case involving a middle-aged woman whose husband shot her during a drinking-related domestic dispute," Waugh recalled.

Felix looked at the woman's body and said, "Funny, how the blood always comes out of the mouth when they've been shot."

Waugh asked his assistant how he knew that.

"Oh, I saw it often when we were fighting on the Russian front," Felix replied.

> We had to take people into the fields, make them dig graves and then shoot them into the graves with machine pistols. They always bled from the mouth like that.

Felix described what he had done "with no more emotion than a farmer might show when talking of slaughtering chickens," Waugh recounted in his startling magazine article.

> Perhaps his peasant background made him an ideal subject for this kind of task. The victims, he told me, were mainly gypsies and Jews who'd been selected by his officers; Felix had simply been a soldier doing as he was ordered.

Early in 1995, Waugh said the controversy over his article eventually died down, and that he had learned that the RCMP did finally manage to track down Felix. But he understood that Felix was not going to be prosecuted because he "is seriously ill in a chronic care institution."

Waugh said that even if Felix's health was good, he would not want to see him brought up on war crimes charges.

"I see him," said Waugh, "as much a victim of his acts as those he killed, and I feel pity and sadness for all."

CHAPTER 28

The Rocket Scientist

When a Lufthansa jet landed in Toronto on July 1, 1990, Immigration Department officials were waiting. Thanks to a tip from Washington, they had a Canada Day surprise for one of the passengers, a retired German rocket scientist named Arthur Rudolph.

They picked him up under a section of the Immigration Act which prohibits suspected war criminals from entering Canada. It was the first time the law had been invoked in the two years since it had been put on the books.

The 83-year-old Rudolph, a meek-looking man with a fringe of white hair circling his mostly bald head, got legal advice and exercised his right to ask for a hearing by an immigration adjudicator, who would decide if there was sufficient reason to bar him from entering Canada.

Rudolph was detained for almost 10 hours. Then, thanks to the Charter of Rights and Freedoms and Canada's remarkably tolerant official attitude toward suspected war criminals, he was released and told he was free to go wherever he pleased in Canada until the hearing could be arranged.

That suited Rudolph just fine.

He had planned to stay for only a month, but ended up spending about six weeks in Canada before returning to his home in Hamburg. By that point, his deportation hearing had already started and the evidence against him was piling up. Rudolph wisely went home of his own accord, although he claimed it was for health and financial reasons, not because he feared he would lose his case.

Rudolph said he had come to Canada to see his daughter, who had flown in from her home in Los Angeles. But some people suspected there was more to it than that.

They thought Rudolph was trying to use Canada in a bid to re-establish himself in the United States, which had been in the process of kicking him out when he voluntarily left six years earlier. According to this theory, Rudolph wanted a Canadian immigration hearing in hopes that he would obtain a favorable ruling. He would then use that ruling as a precedent when he applied for re-entry to the U.S.

Prior to his departure from the States in 1984, Rudolph had lived in the country many years and had become a naturalized citizen. He had a lot of friends in the U.S., and at least one political ally. Congressman James Traficant, a Democrat from Ohio, had introduced a resolution in the U.S. House of Representatives to have the judiciary committee review the Rudolph case, which was unusual, to say the least.

The American government, which had pressured Rudolph into giving up his U.S. citizenship and returning to Germany, had brought him to the States almost 40 years earlier, and taken advantage of his scientific knowledge to help them beat the Russians in the space race.

The Americans recruited Rudolph after the war in what was known as Operation Paperclip. It was a clandestine scheme which brought 118 German scientists to the U.S. to work for both industry and the military. The fact that these skilled people had previously served the Nazis, often in senior positions, was overlooked or covered up by American intelligence.

Eager to recruit these valuable scientists and prevent them from falling into the hands of the Soviets, intelligence officials lied to the State and Immigration departments, which sought to prevent Nazi war criminals from entering the U.S.

Documents which called Rudolph "an ardent Nazi" in 1945 were mysteriously changed, and described him as "not an ardent Nazi" in 1946.

Rudolph was initially employed in the development of the Pershing missile for the U.S. Army. After the establishment of the National Aeronautical and Space Administration, he became chief co-ordinator of the team which developed the Saturn 5 rocket. It was the rocket which put Neil Armstrong and Edwin Aldrin Jr. on the moon in 1969.

Rudolph was highly respected for his work. He shook hands with three U.S. presidents, received medals from both the U.S. Army and NASA, and settled into a comfortable retirement soon after the triumphant first moon landing.

He moved to California, but a threat to his pleasant life emerged a few years later when the U.S. Justice Department started looking for war criminals. In the early 1980s, Nazi-hunters from the Office of Special Investigations started poking into Rudolph's background.

What they found wasn't pretty. Eventually it led to legal action against him, followed by his decision to leave the U.S. voluntarily before he was thrown out.

But soon after his return to Germany, Rudolph started saying publicly that he regretted giving up his American citizenship. He claimed he was not a war criminal, and started working towards his goal of being exonerated and returning to the United States.

Rudolph was not nearly as innocent as he made himself out to be. He had been an early and ardent supporter of Adolf Hitler, joining the Nazi party two years before it came to power in 1933. He was also a member of the SA, the semi-official "brown-shirts" who attacked Jews, communists and others.

But his real crimes were committed after the war started.

Rudolph became production supervisor at a V-2 rocket factory near Nordhausen in central Germany. The rockets were used by the Nazis to terrorize civilians and bomb cities in Britain. The factory where they were built was underground in an old gypsum mine under the Harz Mountains.

The plant was known as Mittelwerk. It was constructed and operated under the supervision of the SS by tens of thousands of inmates from a nearby concentration camp called Dora. These inmates, along with Allied prisoners of war, were forced to dig tunnels, move heavy equipment and perform other back-breaking tasks.

Many of these slave laborers died from malnutrition, overwork, disease and mistreatment. Rudolph later claimed that he didn't know what was going on, but it was hard to imagine that he would not have known since he was in charge of production.

Even worse, he was of high rank, and undoubtedly could have done something to help these poor people if he had wanted to.

Instead, he devoted his energies to building V-2 rockets, and showed no concern for the welfare of the slaves who were used to carry out the task.

Many of the rocket factory laborers suffered from tuberculosis, pneumonia and dysentery, and were forced to work in freezing, dusty conditions for 18-hour shifts, seven days a week. Some 20,000 of the 60,000 prisoners forced to work in the factory died, including many who were hanged or beaten to death for the slightest infraction.

Toward the end, the death rate was so high that the crematorium at the Dora camp was unable to handle the load. The bodies of the many who died were stacked like firewood under stairways. When the Americans arrived at the site near the end of the war, they found the cremation ovens still warm, and hundreds of bodies which the fleeing Nazis had been unable to dispose of.

Rudolph could not have remained ignorant of all this. But at his immigration hearing in Canada in August 1990, he tried to paint himself as the picture of innocence.

He said he didn't know about the Nazi party's anti-semitism until the late 1930s, and that he didn't learn of concentration camp atrocities against Jews until after the war, when he went to the United States.

Rudolph said that when he arrived at Mittelwerk in 1943, he did not know the factory would be underground and would be using forced laborers. Once the factory was operating, he said, he was too busy running the 24-hour, seven-day-a-week operation to notice the thousands of slave laborers who worked for him.

He said the discipline, transportation and feeding of the prisoners was the job of the SS. He testified that he never abused prisoners. While he admitted seeing six prisoners hanged, he said he was not responsible for the hangings.

But a handwriting expert concluded it was probable that Rudolph had signed a document which detailed the conditions under which forced laborers worked in the Heinkel Works in Oranienburg, where Rudolph worked before going to the V-2 plant.

The document, dated April 16, 1943, said the prisoners' work area was surrounded by "five-metre-high towers at certain intervals which are manned by sentries and equipped with floodlights and machine guns." Rudolph claimed he had never seen the document before, let alone signed it.

The immigration hearing continued after Rudolph went back to Germany. Through his lawyer, he continued to fight the expulsion order, but soon a ruling was made, permanently banning him from entry **into** Canada.

Rudolph remained in Germany, but appealed the decision to Federal Court of Appeal. "It is fundamentally wrong and unjust," his lawyer, Barbara Kulaszka, argued.

> He is a German. His country is being devastated and he's trying to help out. How can you say someone like that is a criminal. He worked harder than the prisoners.

But Mr. Justice James Hugessen told Kulaszka that Rudolph was "not merely a foot soldier. He was the manager." The court rejected Rudolph's claim that his exclusion from Canada violated his rights, and concluded there were "reasonable grounds to believe that he was an active participant and accomplice in both war crimes . . . and crimes against humanity."

That was the end of the Rudolph case in Canada, and he never tried to return.

But British journalist Geoffrey Levy tracked him down in Germany in the summer of 1993. Writing in the *Daily Mail*, Levy described his encounter with Rudolph this way:

> He was an old man in a pale blue striped dressing gown and soft, woolly slippers.
>
> But it was his blue eyes you noticed. They were piercingly sharp, alert and nervously watchful for a man of 85. They possessed all the darting instinct for self-survival of a forest animal.
>
> Offered a hand to shake, his own emerged uncertainly through the doorway to take mine briefly and then pull away.
>
> A soft hand, a pink hand that had never wielded anything more physical than a fountain pen while the concentration camp slaves who worked frantically for him were dying of exhaustion or disease, or simply being hanged as an example to others, on one occasion from gantries right outside his office, their mouths stuffed with wood to stop them crying out.

As he had done so many times before, Rudolph denied allegations which were put to him by the journalist. Finally, Rudolph decided he had had enough.

"I am tired of all this," he muttered. "It was a bad time. I have had a bad time. I did my work as a scientist and did not kill anybody. . . . I am an old man. I just want to be left in peace."

At last report, he was living in seclusion in Hamburg.

CHAPTER 29

The Angel and the Orator

Not all the alleged war criminals who came to Canada were Nazis or Nazi collaborators. Of late, some suspected war criminals have arrived in Canada from more recent wars.

Two Africans who settled in Quebec in the early 1990s were linked to atrocities in Rwanda, the scene of a civil war and bloody massacre in which members of the majority Hutu tribe killed members of the minority Tutsi tribe.

In 1994, Canadians saw television pictures of thousands of bloated bodies floating down a Rwandan river.

Protais Zigiranyirazo and Leon Mugesera were alleged to have been among those responsible for as many as a million deaths. Both had close links to the dictator of Rwanda, Juvenal Habyarimana, who was nicknamed "God" because he was all-powerful.

Zigiranyirazo was the dictator's brother-in-law, and one of "God's" so-called "angels," but the tall Hutu was no angel. When rumblings of democracy began in Rwanda in 1990, Zigiranyirazo was part of a group which used violence and intimidation to preserve the dictator's power.

The methods allegedly employed by the Angel would have made Hitler proud.

Zigiranyirazo was said to be chief of the death squads, and reportedly provided soldiers in every region of the country with lists of people to kill. In the beginning, the victims were shot. Later, especially after the dictator himself died when the airplane he was riding in exploded, hundreds of thousands of Tutsis were butchered.

The Angel is a heavyset, arrogant man with dark, beady eyes. He grew up in a rich and powerful family, and as a young man he started climbing his country's political ladder. Eventually he became a diplomat.

After Habyarimana became the dictator in 1973, he appointed the Angel to the position of chief government administrator. He was allegedly involved in the smuggling of cocaine and rare gorilla carcasses.

In his book, *Murders in the Mist*, Nicholas Gordon says the Angel played a part in the death of Dian Fossey in 1984. Fossey was studying the rare mountain gorillas in Rwanda when she was mysteriously killed. Fossey's research was believed to be getting in the way of the Angel's smuggling ring, so he allegedly had her killed.

Zigiranyirazo remained chief government administrator until 1989. The next year, he and his wife and their three children moved to Montreal, where the Angel attended classes in political science at the University of Quebec.

He made frequent trips home. It's believed that during these trips he presided at meetings of the death squads.

The most solid evidence of this came in a report released in 1994. The report, issued by an international commission of inquiry into human rights abuses in Rwanda, said the Angel took part in a 1991 meeting at which top government officials, including the dictator, planned mass killings.

The Angel's presence in Canada went largely unnoticed until he got into trouble with some of his fellow-Rwandans who had come to Canada as refugees.

Apparently upset that the refugees were blaming him for the genocide in Rwanda, the Angel uttered death threats against them. Two exiled human rights activists, Fidele Makombe and Jean Paul Kimonyo, complained about these threats, and the Angel was forced to appear in court.

Makombe and Kimonyo, both in their 30s, said they were walking through a metro station when they heard a voice behind them uttering threats. When they turned, they discovered that it was the Angel.

Kimonyo testified: "He saw us and told us, 'You better stop doing this to me, or I will do to you what I am doing at home.' "

The Angel's relationship with Makombe was a complex one. The accused man testified that he often ate at Makombe's home, and that he and Makombe often went for walks together. The Angel claimed he was godfather to Makombe's nephew. Makombe admitted this, but denied any other contact with the man.

The Angel was convicted. The judge said he found Zigiranyirazo's testimony "evasive, hesitant and contradictory," and told the unfazed defendant there was no place in Canada for threats.

The Angel got off with a suspended sentence, and he was never tried in Canada for war crimes. Following his conviction for uttering the death threats, he returned to Rwanda. When he came back to Canada, he was arrested for entering the country with a criminal record. Days later, the Angel was deported and told he could never return.

Zigiranyirazo is now believed to be living in an African country. If he ever returns to his homeland, he will probably join 12,000 other Rwandans who have been charged with war crimes. Given the nature of the allegations against him, it's likely he would be sentenced to death.

Montreal lawyer William Schabas summed things up nicely with respect to the Angel: "Canada has a long history of being a haven to war criminals," he observed, "so this isn't the first case and probably won't be the last."

He was right.

Leon Mugesera, the second suspected Rwandan war criminal who settled in the province of Quebec, soon came to public attention. As this book went to press, the Canadian government was trying to deport Mugesera.

He was arrested early in 1995 under a section of the Immigration Act which targets people who are believed to have committed crimes against humanity. As well, he was accused of concealing the fact that he faced criminal charges in Rwanda when he applied for admission to Canada.

Mugesera was born in Rwanda in 1952 into a middle-class family. He was intelligent and won many scholarships. Because of his superior education, Mugesera was a natural for politics. He soon became political advisor to the Rwandan dictator.

He gave a speech in November 1992 which was broadcast on Rwandan radio. In that speech, Mugesera allegedly called on the nation's Hutus to kill Tutsis. He also allegedly called for the execution of anyone who was against the dictator's rule, and for the decimation of those who supported the Tutsi-dominated Rwandan Patriotic Front.

At the time, the RPF was the major opposition party. Currently the RPF is the ruling party in Rwanda, and if the people now in power get their hands of Mugesera, they will likely show him no mercy.

"The fatal error we made in '59, when I was still a child," Mugesera reportedly said in his speech, "was that we let them leave." This was a reference to the mass exodus of Tutsis from Rwanda following a Hutu nationalist uprising in 1959.

"What are we waiting for to decimate these families and the people who recruit them?" he asked rhetorically in his speech. "Are you sincerely going to wait for them to come and decimate you?"

Later in the speech, Mugesera allegedly said that Tutsis were foreigners with Ethiopian roots. He allegedly said they should be sent back to Ethiopia, and suggested that "we would find them a shortcut – that is, the Nyabarongo River."

About eight months later, right after the dictator's death in 1992, Mugesera's reported suggestions began to be carried out. The river was soon filled with the bodies of Tutsis, but by that time Mugesera had fled.

Exactly what he said in the speech is the subject of much dispute at his deporation hearing in Canada. After he gave his controversial speech, his political career was cut short. Even in Rwanda, the speech was too extreme. The day after he gave the speech, a warrant for his arrest was issued and he was fired as political advisor.

The ill-fated orator spent the next month hiding in a military camp, where civilian law couldn't touch him. Then he somehow managed to sneak into Spain, where he convinced the Canadian embassy that he was a refugee.

IIe was granted admission to Canada, and soon arrived in Quebec City with his wife and five children. He studied linguistics at Laval University and was given landed immigrant status in 1993. But the following year, the federal government found that an international human rights mission that included Canadians, Americans, Europeans and Africans had named Mugesera as one of the high-level officials calling for Tutsi deaths.

As well, a senior official of the RPF rebel movement testified before a House of Commons committee in Ottawa that Mugesera planned the killing of Tutsis.

RCMP and immigration officials soon came to Mugesera's modest Sainte-Foy apartment, where they arrested him and took him to a Montreal prison. Much to the dismay of many Rwandans living in Canada, Mugesera was let out on just $5,000 bail while he awaited his deportation hearing.

"I don't know if you can understand what this man represents to us," said Jean Kamanzi, president of the Association of Canadians of Origin in Rwanda, shortly after Mugesera's arrest. "I think the only people who can really understand what we're feeling are the Jews. It's just as though they knew of a Nazi living in Canada."

Alison Des Forges, a member of the human rights group known as Africa Watch, concluded that the way the Hutus killed the Tutsis was very much like the way the Nazis killed the Jews.

"It's basically the same kind of politics that Hitler used against the Jews," she said, "to unite the majority against a minority by saying these are vile betrayers of the motherland, and they deserve to die."

CHAPTER 30

A Legal Strip Tease

The 50th anniversary of the end of the Second World War might have been a good time for Ottawa to stop chasing old Nazi war criminals. It was a costly and largely unsuccessful venture, and it had to end sometime.

Logically, the 50-year mark was a sensible quitting point. But logic takes second place to anger and other emotions when it comes to Nazi war criminals, particularly as far as Jewish people are concerned.

To most Jews, the fact that 50 years had passed meant that torturers and murderers who took part in the Holocaust had gotten away with their crimes for a half-century. The significance of the 50-year mark was that time was running out. They felt that every effort must be made in the coming years to identify and punish surviving Nazi monsters, before they permanently cheated justice by dying.

So the federal government decided to keep up the chase. Early in 1995, as the nation prepared to celebrate the anniversary of the end of the war, the government renewed its commitment to prosecute suspected Nazi war criminals.

Timing their statements to coincide with the 50th anniversary of the Russian liberation of the Auschwitz death camp in Poland, Justice Minister Allan Rock and Immigration Minister Sergio Marchi announced that they had their sights set on no fewer than a dozen new suspects. They said their departments were teaming up to kick these people out of Canada.

They played down the fact that Ottawa was abandoning efforts to bring suspects before the criminal courts, where accused persons have maximum legal rights. Instead, prosecutors were going to try to strip war criminals of their naturalized Canadian citizenship, and then deport them.

So it was back to D and D again. That was the method used for many years by the Americans, and that was the method used in Canada against Jacob Luitjens (see Chapter 24) in the government's only successful war crimes prosecution to date.

The size of the government's 1995 initiative was surprising. People wondered how a dozen new suspects could have been discovered, still alive after so many years had passed. Had the government been sitting on the files of all these alleged war criminals, waiting to make a big 50th anniversary splash?

People wanted to know who the 12 suspects were. They wanted details of the allegations, and they wondered what the suspects had to say for themselves. But that's when strange things started happening, and it wasn't long before it became clear that the big Rock-Marchi initiative was long on promises and short on action.

As things turned out, it was not going to be a blockbuster event that would be a massive and quick effort to rid the nation of surviving Nazi war criminals. Instead, these cases were going to be trotted out, one by one, over the next several years, enabling the government to milk each case for maximum publicity. Ottawa was going to engage in a sort of legal strip-tease.

One by one, the suspects were going to be paraded before the public and held up as proof that no matter how much time had passed, the government was still "doing something" about Nazi war criminals in Canada. The government had stocked its basket with a dozen eggs. There would always be a fresh case to cite as proof that something was being done.

After the big announcement, prosecutors refused to identify any of the 12 suspects, saying that their names would come out in due course, as denaturalization and deportation actions against them began making their way through the legal system.

And so the legal strip-tease began.

Prosecutors said that only four of the cases would be proceeded with initially. Action against the other eight would be deferred until the government got a sense of how things would go with the first four. How long might that take? No one could say. Meanwhile, of course, time was passing.

As Frank Diamont, executive vice-president of B'nai Brith, pointed out:

> It has taken us 50 years and we are still getting piecemeal justice in Canada. The biological clock is ticking rapidly. We just don't have the time to waste.

But the government did have time to waste. It wasn't until two months after the Rock-Marchi announcement that the first of the 12 suspects was identified. He turned out to be a Toronto man named Erichs Tobiass, a Latvian immigrant who had been in Canada for 44 years.

When his name was announced, reporters rushed to the tan brick bungalow where Tobiass, a frail widower whose only companion was a black cat, had lived since 1957.

When a reporter asked him to comment, Tobiass said: "I have nothing to say or nothing to talk about." Then the 84-year-old man shut his door, avoided the press, and quietly awaited developments.

Tobiass was a retired auto mechanic. His neighbors rarely saw him, except when he made the occasional trip to the store in his large, well-kept car, or worked in his garden. People described him as a "very quiet and clean man" and a "good guy." One neighbor astutely pointed out that Tobiass was so old, "there is not much man left to deport."

But the government was eager to take away his citizenship and deport him, despite his advanced age. Prosecutors said they intended to call 54 witnesses, most of them from Germany, Israel, Britain and the United States. In addition, the government said it would present about 150 documents in court, giving the impression that there was an overwhelming amount of evidence against Tobiass.

The prosecution claimed that during the war, Tobiass was a member of the Latvian Auxiliary Security Police, which was also known as the Arajs Commando. The government said that between 1941 and 1943, Tobiass's duties included serving as a chauffeur for high-ranking Arajs Commando members and German officers.

According to documents filed by the government in Federal Court, Tobiass had previously admitted being involved "in an active capacity" in two executions in the summer of 1941.

The Arajs Commando was deemed to be responsible for the deaths of about 30,000 Latvian Jews. It also rounded up, interrogated and executed partisans and communists. On one day in

March 1941, the unit allegedly shot and killed 153 old and sick people. In one week of the same year, the unit was reported to have shot 633 people, seized 234 others for slave labor and burned 31 villages.

The prosecutors alleged that Tobiass was actively involved in such activities. From January to March 1943, the government claimed, Tobiass was a member of a team which killed hundreds of suspected partisans and burned villages. Between 1943 and 1945, the prosecution said, Tobiass was a member of the German security police or Waffen SS, and by 1944 he was a sergeant.

According to the government, Tobiass fled Latvia with the Waffen SS in April 1945 and entered a German DP camp, where he lived for two years before travelling to England. In 1951, he arrived in Halifax. Six years later, after he had settled in the Toronto suburb of North York, he became a Canadian citizen.

As this book was going to press in the autumn of 1995, the Tobiass case was still before the Federal Court. But a potentially serious flaw in the government's case was apparent. It turned out that the government had known about Tobiass and his alleged war crimes for 29 years before legal action was taken against him.

Why had the authorities waited until 1995 before prosecuting him? It was a pertinent question, in view of the provision in the Canadian Charter of Rights and Freedoms guaranteeing a speedy trial to a person accused of committing a crime. It was almost certain that the defence would argue that the government had violated Tobiass's constitutional rights by waiting so long to bring him to court.

Back in 1966, the government had been informed that Tobiass was a suspected war criminal. Nazi hunter Simon Wiesenthal had sent a letter containing Tobiass's name, a Toronto address, and allegations that he was a war criminal, to the Canadian ambassador in Vienna. The ambassador, Margaret Meagher, passed the information on to Ottawa.

Documents examined in the National Archives by Sol Littman of the Simon Wiesenthal Centre's Canadian office showed that Ambassador Meagher waited eight months for a reply from Ottawa. She was finally told that further communication with Wiesenthal was not a good idea, "because if you do, he may expect that we will do something."

This response was in keeping with the government's policy at that time of doing nothing about suspected war criminals in

Canada. But members of Canada's Jewish community weren't willing to let the matter drop. In late 1966, they sent the government a letter listing various suspected war criminals, once again fingering Tobiass. And once again, the government chose not to act.

The reply from a government official to the Jewish community was curt: "Thank you very much for the information," he said, "I wish you a Happy New Year."

Why did the government wait until almost 30 years later to prosecute Tobiass? Did his name come up during the Deschênes investigation in the mid-1980s? If it did, why did the government wait for a decade after that to take him to court? These and many more questions remain to be answered.

In April 1995, a month after the Tobiass case began, the government identified the second of the 12 suspects. He was Joseph Nemsila, who was accused of lying to immigration officials decades earlier, when he had entered Canada.

The 82-year-old Nemsila looked like a relatively easy target, since he had never taken out Canadian citizenship, and was liable to deportation without first having to be denaturalized. He held only landed immigrant status, and could be taken quickly before an immigration adjudicator in a bid to kick him out of Canada.

The government was prepared to call 25 witnesses and offer some 200 documents to make its case. Prosecutors claimed that Nemsila had lied about being a member of the Hlinka Guard in his native Slovakia during the war.

But the case fell apart almost immediately.

Immigration adjudicator Ed McNamara ruled that Nemsila was protected from deportation by a law dating back to 1910. That law said that a landed immigrant who had been in the country for five years could not be deported, whether or not he had entered Canada under false pretences, unless he had committed treason or drug offences.

Although that 1910 law was taken off the books in 1978, McNamara ruled that it still protected Nemsila, because it was in effect when he acquired "domicile" status in Canada in 1955, five years after he came to Canada.

For his part, Nemsila insisted that even if the old law had not protected him, he still couldn't be deported, because he had told immigration officials that he had been a member of the Hlinka Guard, and they let him into Canada anyway. He maintained in a

CTV interview that during the war, he had only done his patriotic duty.

"My order was to go against the uprisers and put the uprisers down," he said. "I am not guilty. I am not involved personally in anything, in anything. You must understand that."

Nemsila claimed that Canada's Jewish community was behind the attempt to deport him. "The Jews, the Jews, they will never change," he said. "If it will not stop me, it will go further. They will go after other people."

About 10 days after Nemsila was publicly accused, the third of the 12 suspects was identified. He was Helmut Oberlander, who at 71 was relatively young. A home-builder from Waterloo, Ontario, Oberlander was a German who arrived in Canada in 1954.

The government accused him of failing to tell immigration officials that he had been a member of a Nazi mobile killing unit responsible for executing thousands of Jews during the war. Through his lawyer, Robert McGee, Oberlander denied the allegations. At press time, his case was still before the courts.

The fourth of the 12 suspects was a man from St. Catharines, Ontario. Johann Dueck, 76, had cancer and had been told by doctors that he had only about two years to live. He was accused of not telling immigration officials of his alleged participation in the execution of civilians and prisoners of war while a member of the Selidovka district police in German-occupied Ukraine between 1941 and 1943.

Dueck went to Australia after the war, and arrived in Canada in 1948. He became a citizen in 1957 and settled in St. Catharines soon after that. He worked as a contractor and mechanic.

His local Member of Parliament, Walt Lastewka, expressed support for Dueck. "I feel very uncomfortable that we have to go back 50 years to correct whatever happened then," Lastewka said. The MP was quickly criticized by members of the Jewish community for his politically incorrect remarks. Lastewka was accused of giving the impression that it was wrong to pursue suspected war criminals, no matter how long ago their alleged offences had been committed. To many Jews, saying that was equivalent to being anti-semitic.

Dueck's lawyer, Donald Bayne – who had successfully defended Michael Pawlowski after he was charged in 1989 with murdering 400 Jews in Belarus (see Chapters 22 and 23) – said Dueck would welcome a chance to face charges in criminal court, because he was an innocent man.

Bayne accused the government of abandoning its commitment to file criminal charges against alleged Nazi war criminals, in favor of what he termed the more "politically expedient" option of denaturalization and deportation proceedings. At press time, the Dueck case was also still before the courts.

And what about the remaining eight suspects of the 12 on the government's 1995 hit list? Presumably they will trickle out into the public domain over the coming months and years. And conceivably, there could still be more cases after that.

Simon Wiesenthal recently estimated that more than 160,000 people were directly involved in committing war crimes or acted as accomplices. "If you consider the non-German Nazi collaborators in all parts of Europe," Wiesenthal said, "the number would reach maybe 200,000. Around the world, there are 15,000 to 20,000 who are still alive."

If Wiesenthal is right, a fair number of suspected Nazi war criminals are still living in Canada. If the government decides to keep chasing them until the last one is dead, they could well be making headlines and court appearances into the 21st century.

Josef Mengele

CHAPTER NOTES

Chapters 1 and 2

The main source for these chapters was *Meeting of Generals* by Tony Foster. Also useful was *The Trial of Kurt Meyer* by B.J.S. MacDonald.

An article by Ralph Allen in the Feb. 1, 1950, issue of *Maclean's* headlined "Was Kurt Meyer Guilty?" was also useful.

Chapter 3

This chapter was based on materials I examined in the Public Archives in Ottawa. The transcripts of the three trials discussed in this chapter are kept in Records Group 25 F3, volumes 2608 and 2609.

Chapter 4

This chapter was the first of many I researched primarily by using the Lexis-Nexis electronic database, which contains archival material from hundreds of newspapers, magazines and other publications.

Using a modem, I was able to bring up relevant articles onto the screen of my desktop computer. Especially useful for this chapter was a piece by Bill Schiller titled "Hitler's Last General," which appeared in *The Toronto Star* on June 5, 1994.

Chapter 5

The unpublished historical background report prepared by Alti Rodal for the Deschênes commission was most helpful in preparing this chapter. It was titled *Nazi War Criminals in Canada: The Historical and Policy Setting from the 1940s to the Present*. In particular, the quotes from Ethyl Ostry's diary are taken from Rodal's report.

An article titled "Canada used loose screen to filter Nazi fugitives" by Reg Whitaker from *The Globe and Mail's* March 1, 1985, issue was informative.

My visit to France and Germany in May 1994 also enabled me to get a clearer sense of what went on during the post-war years, and was helpful in writing the first five chapters of the book.

Chapter 6

An article titled "Barbie's Buddy in Canada" by Sol Littman in the October 1987 edition of *Canadian Dimension* magazine was a good beginning. Searches on Lexis-Nexis yielded several other articles. Especially informative were two which ran on Sept. 24, 1994 in the Montreal *Gazette*. They were titled "Phony count oversaw the massacres of Resistance fighters" and "Pro-fascist groups active in the 1940s."

Chapter 7

This chapter was based in part on the Deschênes commission report and on Alti Rodal's historical background report (mentioned above).

Also useful was Sol Littman's article titled "The Ukrainian Halychyna Division: A Case Study of Historical Revisionism," which appeared in a handbook on Holocaust literature.

I also obtained information from the book titled *Old Wounds: Jews, Ukrainians and the Hunt for Nazi War Criminals in Canada*.

Chapter 8

The main source for this chapter was a long article titled "War Criminals in Canada: The issue that won't go away" published in the Aug. 28, 1982, edition of *Today* magazine.

Chapter 9

Journalism student Lisa Cook was the primary researcher for this chapter. Her main source was "The Kirschbaum File," a tabloid supplement put out by the Kingston *Whig-Standard* on Dec. 10, 1988. The supplement was researched and written by Paul McKay.

Additional information was drawn from *The Los Angeles Times*, the CTK National News Wire, and a letter written by Burnett M. Thall to Sol Littman of the Simon Wiesenthal Centre.

Chapter 10

Journalism student Brian Miller was the principal researcher for this chapter. He began with the book *Justice Not Vengeance* by Simon Wiesenthal, which contains a chapter on Hermine Braunsteiner Ryan. Then he used Lexis-Nexis to turn up news articles from Reuters news agency, United Press International, *Time* magazine and *The Christian Science Monitor*.

He used The New York Times Index to find articles which appeared in that paper from July 14, 1964 to Sept. 23, 1972.

Chapter 11

Journalism student Deb Hadley was the primary researcher for this chapter. Her methodology included a search of the Lexis-Nexis database. In addition, she used articles from *The Globe and Mail*, *The Worcester (Mass.) Telegram* and *The Calgary Herald*, as well as *Alberta Report* magazine. She covered the period from June 1984 to June 1985.

Chapter 12

Journalism student Denise Psiurski did the research for this chapter. Her major sources were *The Winnipeg Free Press* (August and September 1960; March 1961; and February 1990 and 1991), *The New York Times* (Sept. 1960 and March 1961), *The Globe and Mail* (Sept. 1960 and April 1991).

She also used the books *Forged in Fury* by Michael Elkins and *Web of Hate* by Warren Kinsella.

In addition, she conducted telephone interviews with Arthur Drache, Gisela Herzl, Elizabeth Steinlauf, Fred Woodward and Keith Rutherford.

Chapter 13

The chief source of information for this chapter was a personal interview with Dymtro Kupyak.

Additional material was drawn from Kupyak's book, *Memoirs of One Not Slain*, as well as from a Soviet "special bulletin on war criminals," and from a Soviet affidavit."

Newspaper reports were also helpful, especially those published right after Kupyak was accused of being a war criminal on Oct. 23, 1964.

Chapter 14

The main source for this chapter was Sol Littman's book, *War Criminal on Trial: The Rauca Case*. Also helpful were articles from United Press International and *The New York Times*, as well as transcripts of court proceedings against Albert Helmut Rauca.

Chapter 15

The major sources of information were *Quiet Neighbors: Prosecuting Nazi War Criminals in America* by Alan A. Ryan Jr. and "The Unorthodox Rabbi," an article by Sheldon Teitelbaum and Tom Waldman in the July 15, 1990, issue of the *Los Angeles Times* magazine.

Chapter 16

The Deschênes commission report provided much of the information for this chapter, along with newspaper reports, particularly those from *The Toronto Star* in January and February 1985.

Additional material was drawn from news releases sent out by the Simon Wiesenthal Centre, and from an interview with Sol Littman.

The library at the Canadian Jewish Congress offices in Toronto also had a good file of newspaper clippings on Mengele.

Chapters 17 and 18

The major source for these chapters was the Deschênes commission report. The article quoting General Burns was headlined, "Should Losing General Be Hanged?" It appeared in the Jan. 26, 1952, issue of *Saturday Night*.

Chapter 19

The source of this material was the historical background report prepared by Alti Rodal for the Deschênes commission. It was titled *Nazi War Criminals in Canada: The Historical and Policy Setting from the 1940s to the Present*.

Chapters 20 and 21

The Finta case received extensive news coverage, especially between the time of his arrest on Dec. 9, 1987, until the release of the Supreme Court of Canada's ruling on March 23, 1994.

I found articles by Paul Lungen in *The Canadian Jewish News* to be particularly complete and insightful. (I also interviewed Lungen and the newspaper's editor, Patricia Rucker, about the Finta case and related matters.)

Maclean's magazine also had good coverage of the Finta case.

The judgment issued by the Ontario Court of Appeal upholding Finta's acquittal was quite useful.

My visit to Hungary in May 1994, also gave me valuable background and insight. In particular, the Jewish Museum in Budapest was a rich source of information.

Chapter 22 and 23

I used stories from many newspapers in these chapters. The Pawlowski case received extensive coverage from the time of his arrest on Dec. 18, 1989, until the final group of charges were dropped on June 10, 1991.

The case was covered not only by the major news organizations, but the Renfrew *Mercury*, Pawlowski's hometown paper, which provided interesting material not picked up by the big dailies.

I also used the press release issued Jan. 3, 1990, by the U.S.S.R. embassy, along with various documents filed with the Supreme Court of Ontario. The most useful of these were the lengthy and detailed judgment issued by Mr. Justice James Chadwick on June 21, 1991.

Chapter 24

Press coverage was also extensive in the Luitjens case from the time Ottawa started legal procedings against him on March 16, 1988 until he was deported on Nov. 26, 1992. *The Vancouver Sun* provided especially detailed coverage.

The judgment issued by Mr. Justice Frank Collier of the Federal Court of Canada on Oct. 22, 1991, was also very useful.

Chapter 25

Newspaper reports on the Reistetter case were the main source of information for this chapter. *The St. Catharines Standard* provided especially good coverage from the time the suspect was arrested on Jan. 18, 1990, until the charges were dropped on March 4, 1991.

Chapter 26

The Windsor Star provided the best news coverage on the Grujicic case, starting with the time of his arrest on Dec. 8, 1992, but I used articles from several other papers as well to research this chapter.

The most valuable and interesting sources of information were court documents. On Sept. 27, 1994, Mr. Justice William Donnelly released his judgment, ending the prosecution of Grujicic. Attached to that ruling were several "schedules" which provided insight into Grujicic's life in Yugoslavia, his secret involvement with the RCMP and other matters.

Chapter 27

This chapter is based on "Down in the morgue," an article by Dr. Douglas Waugh in the April 1993 issue of the *Canadian Medical Association Journal.*

Additional material came from a phone interview with Waugh by journalism student Brian Miller.

Chapter 28

Day-by-day coverage of the events while Rudolph was in Canada were obtained mainly from *The Toronto Star* (July and August 1990.) Additional information came from the ruling of the Federal Court of Appeal in the Rudolph case, released May 1, 1992.

Other information was obtained from articles which appeared in American and British newspapers. These included *The Los Angleles Times* ("A Matter of Conscience or Convenience?" Sept. 3, 1990); *The Daily Telegraph* ("Inside Hitler's Death Tunnels," June 5, 1993); and the *Daily Mail* ("I Was Only Obeying Orders," June 19, 1993).

Chapter 29

Journalism student Justin Kohlman did the majority of the research for this chapter. The Montreal *Gazette* from 1993 to 1995 was his chief resource.

Other information was drawn from *The Globe and Mail, Times* Newspapers, Canadian Press, *U.S. News and World Report* magazine, and the book *Murder in the Mist: Who killed Dian Fossey?* by Nicholas Gordon.

Telephone interviews were conducted with Rwandan immigrants Jean-Paul Kimonyo and Fidele Makombe, and Alexander Norris of the Montreal *Gazette*.

Chapter 30

Journalism student Michelle Spencer was the primary researcher for the material on Erichs Tobiass in this chapter. Her main sources were *The Globe and Mail* from August 1994 to April 1995, and *The Toronto Star* from March 1995 to April 1995, as well as Southam News and *The Washington Post*. Southam News and *The Toronto Star* were the main sources for the information on the other suspected war criminals discussed in this chapter.

She also conducted telephone interviews with Paul Lungen of the *Canadian Jewish News*, Peter Kremer, head of the Justice Department's war crimes unit, Stephen Bindman of Southam News, Rudy Platiel of *The Globe and Mail* and Jack Silverstone of the Canadian Jewish Congress.

Dymtro Kupyak

SELECTED BIBLIOGRAPHY

Aarons, Mark. *Sanctuary! Nazi Fugitives in Australia.* William Heinemann, 1989.

Abella, Irving and Harold Troper. *None Is Too Many.* Lester & Orpen Dennys, 1983.

Ashman, Charles and Robert J. Wagman. *The Nazi Hunters: The Shocking True Story of the Continuing Search for Nazi War Criminals.* Pharos Books, 1988.

Berenbaum, Michael. *The World Must Know.* Little, Brown and Company, 1993.

Blum, Howard. *Wanted! The Search for Nazis in America.* Quadrangle/The New York Times Book Co., 1977.

Browning, Christopher R. *Ordinary Men: Reserve Police Battalion 101 and the Final Solution in Poland.* Harper Perennial, 1993.

Brym, Robert J., William Shaffir and Morton Weinfeld. *The Jews in Canada.* Oxford University Press, 1993.

Deschênes, Jules. *Commission of Inquiry on War Criminals Report, Part 1: Public.* Ministry of Supply and Services, 1987.

Dollinger, Hans. *The Decline and Fall of Nazi Germany and Imperial Japan.* Bonanza Books, 1965.

Elkins, Michael. *Forged in Fury.* Ballantine Books, 1971.

Epstein, Helen. *Children of the Holocaust.* G. P. Putnam's Sons, 1979.

Fest, Joachim C. *The Face of the Third Reich.* Penguin Books, 1979.

Foster, Tony. *Meeting of Generals.* Methuen Publications, 1986.

Gilbert, G. M. *Nuremberg Diary.* New American Libary, 1947.

Gilbert, Martin. *The Illustated Atlas of Jewish Civilization.* Collier MacMillan, 1990.

Gordon, Nicholas. *Murder in the Mist: Who killed Dian Fossey?* Kent, Hodder and Stoughton, 1994.

Kinsella, Warren. *Web of Hate.* Harper Collins, 1994.

Kupyak, Dymtro. *Memoirs of One Not Slain.* Beskyd Graphics, 1991.

Lipstadt, Deborah. *Denying the Holocaust: The Growing Assault on Truth and Memory*. Macmillan, 1993.

Littman, Sol. *War Criminal on Trial: The Rauca Case*. Lester & Orpen Dennys, 1983.

Loftus, John. *The Belarus Secret: The Nazi Connection in America*. Paragon House, 1989.

MacDonald, B.J.S. *The Trial of Kurt Meyer*. Clarke, Irwin, 1954.

Matas, David, with Susan Charendoff. *Justice Delayed: Nazi War Criminals in Canada*. Summerhill Press, 1987.

Rodal, Alti. *Nazi War Criminals in Canada: The Historical and Policy Setting from the 1940s to the Present*. Unpublished, part of the Deschênes commission research material, 1986.

Ryan, Allan A., Jr. *Quiet Neighbors: Prosecuting Nazi War Criminals in America*. Harcourt Brace Jovanovich, 1984.

Sopinka, John. *Ukrainian-Canadian Committee Submission to the Commission of Inquiry on War Criminals*. Justinian Press, 1986.

Taylor, A.J.P. *History of World War II*. Octopus Books, 1974.

Time-Life Books, the editors of. *World War II: The Aftermath – Europe*. Time-Life Books, 1976.

Time-Life Books, the editors of. *WW II: History of the Second World War*. Prentice Hall, 1989.

Toland, John. *The Last 100 Days*. Random House, 1966.

Tolstoy, Nikolai. *Trial and Error: Canada's Commission of Inquiry on War Criminals and the Soviets*. Justinian Press, 1986.

Troper, Harold and Morton Weinfeld. *Old Wounds: Jews, Ukrainians and the Hunt for Nazi War Criminals in Canada*. Viking, 1988.

Urwin, Derek W. *Western Europe Since 1945: A Political History*. Longman, 1989.

Wiesenthal, Simon. *Justice Not Vengeance*. Usidenfeld and Nicolson, 1989.

Wiesenthal, Simon. *The Murderers Among Us*. McGraw-Hill, 1967.

INDEX OF NAMES